A Comparison of World Religions

BY

HENRY J. HEYDT, TH.D.

CHRISTIAN LITERATURE CRUSADE

FORT WASHINGTON PENNSYLVANIA 19034

CHRISTIAN LITERATURE CRUSADE

U.S.A.
Box 1449, Fort Washington, PA 19034

CANADA
Box 189, Elgin, Ontario KOG 1EO

GREAT BRITAIN
51 The Dean, Alresford, Hants., SO24 9BJ

AUSTRALIA
P.O. Box 91, Pennant Hills, N.S.W. 2120

ISBN 0-87508-241-6

This printing 1989

PRINTED IN THE UNITED STATES OF AMERICA

A Comparison of World Religions

CHRONOLOGY OF THE ELEVEN MAJOR RELIGIONS*

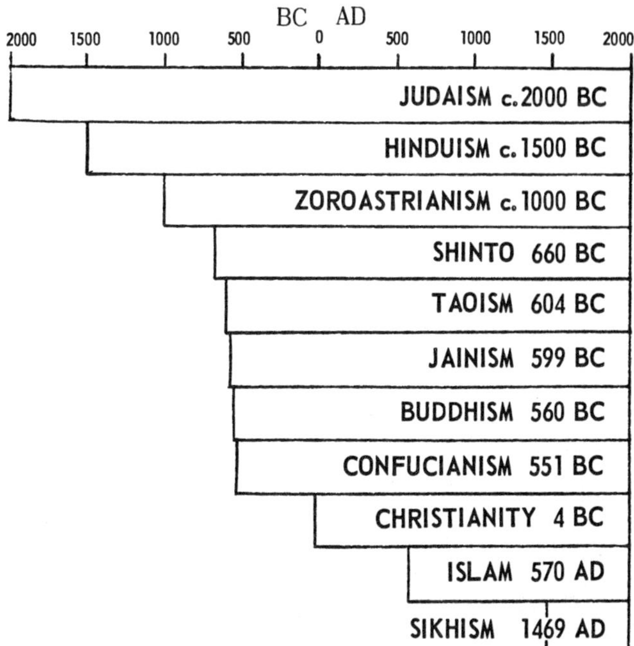

*Birth dates of the founders are used where possible.

Contents

INTRODUCTION 9

CHAPTER I Historical Survey 11
Judaism 12
Christianity 15
Hinduism 17
Zoroastrianism 19
Shinto 20
Taoism 23
Jainism 25
Buddhism 27
Confucianism 29
Islam 30
Sikhism 32

CHAPTER II Sacred Literature 35
Judaism 36
Christianity 41
Hinduism 45
Zoroastrianism 54
Shinto 56
Taoism 58
Jainism 60
Buddhism 61
Confucianism 64
Islam 66
Sikhism 70

CHAPTER III Topical Comparison 73
Deities Worshipped 73
Belief Concerning Sin 76
Method of Salvation 77
Belief Concerning the Future Life 80
The Golden Rule 84
Liberality 86

CHAPTER IV Distinctives of Christianity 91
The Distinctive Features of Christianity 91
The Distinctive Person of Christianity 92
The Distinctive Book of Christianity 99
The Distinctive Doctrine of Christianity 106

BIBLIOGRAPHY 111

Introduction

Creation itself bears witness to the Creator, and man in the beginning knew God. However, he glorified Him not as God, was not thankful, became vain in his reasonings, and his senseless heart was darkened. He changed the glory of God into gods of his own devising, so God gave him up to his own lusts (Rom. 1:20–32). Religion is therefore not an evolution from polytheism to monotheism but a degeneration from monotheism to polytheism. Elements of the true knowledge of God once known to man are even yet found in world religions, sometimes in grossly perverted forms, but indicating the light that was once known.

We shall limit the scope of this study to extant religions only, and out of these we shall select simply those that have coherent expression. The unsystematized religious expressions of savage tribes disappear when they come into contact with the concrete faiths that have survived the centuries. We shall also exclude Mormonism and Christian Science even though they have their sacred books, since they belong more properly to the study of cults.

Eleven faiths will be compared. Of these, four are listed as monotheistic: Judaism, Christianity,

Islam, and Sikhism. Zoroastrianism approaches monotheism but has a strain of dualism. The rest are essentially polytheistic. Chapter One will give a brief historical survey of each, based primarily upon *Webster's New International Dictionary*. Entire sections taken from *Webster* will be indicated by quotation marks. Chapter Two will give the sacred scriptures of each, including quotations from all, with the exception of Judaism and Christianity, since their Scriptures are readily available. Chapter Three will give a topical comparison of the teachings of these faiths. Chapter Four will deal with the distinctiveness of Christianity.

It remains for us to declare our attitude to religious faiths other than our own. It is understandable that each considers his own the truth faith. This is a logical necessity. But are we to condemn all the rest? What place shall we give them? We recognize that there are elements of good and truth in all faiths, but this does not mean that they are acceptable to God. They are all bridges broken at the other end. They cannot save. This applies to Judaism also since its rejection of the Lord Jesus Christ, for He alone is the way, the truth, and the life, and no man comes to the Father but through Him (John 14:6). This accounts for the strong missionary aspect of Christianity. It also constitutes an incentive to study other faiths so that, like Paul in the Areopagus, we can intelligently point their adherents to Christ (Acts 17:22–31). The Christian will also come into a fuller understanding and appreciation of his own faith by a comparative study.

Chapter One

Historical Survey

A survey of this nature may be pursued in a variety of ways. Some prefer to classify religions as universal and non-universal. Others study them according to their geographical origins, the number of their adherents, the number of recognized deities, and so forth. We shall arrange them chronologically, using the birth dates, where possible, of their founders.

We begin with Judaism. Some have wrongly listed the origin of Judaism as beginning with Moses. This would constitute Hinduism an older faith than Judaism by approximately five hundred years. It was Abraham, however, who was the progenitor of the Chosen People, and the Jews to this day trace their descent to him. Furthermore, the Hebrew Scriptures themselves go back beyond Abraham to creation itself, and trace the descent of Abraham from the very first man. According to its own Scriptures, therefore, Judaism is not only the oldest extant religion, but the oldest of all religions.

Christianity is listed next because it is connected with Judaism not only historically but, we believe, inextricably. Leo Eddleman, in his book *The Teachings of Jesus,* correctly states, "Christianity is the flower of which Judaism is the bud. What the Jews... and some Christians ... fail to grasp is that pure Judaism is embryonic Christianity and genuine Christianity is Judaism full-grown." Sufficient evidence of this is seen in the one fact alone that the Christian Scriptures embrace the entire thirty-nine books of the Hebrew Sacred Canon.

JUDAISM

The word "Judaism" is derived from the Latin *Judaismus* which in turn comes from the Greek *Ioudaismos.* This is translated "the Jews' religion" in Galatians 1, verses 13 and 14, the only occurrences in the New Testament. The verb *ioudaizo* occurs in Galatians 2:14 where it is translated "to live as do the Jews." The term "Judaism" was first used about 100 B.C. and is found twice in Maccabees:

> Now the things concerning Judas Maccabaeus and his brethren, and the purification of the great temple, and the dedication of the altar, and further the wars against Antiochus Epiphanes, and Eupator his son, and the manifestations that came from heaven unto those that vied with one another in manful deeds

> for the religion of the Jews (II Maccabees 2:20–22).
>
> But Judas, who is also called Maccabaeus, and they that were with him, making their way privily into the villages, called unto them their kinsfolk; and taking unto them such as had continued in the Jews' religion, gathered together as many as six thousand (II Maccabees 8:1).

The Jews are a Semitic people since they are descendants of Shem. Abraham was designated "the Hebrew" (Gen. 14:13) and therefore those descendants of Shem through Abraham are called Hebrews. The name "Israel" was conferred upon Jacob, the son of Isaac and grandson of Abraham (Gen. 32:28), and came to be used for all the Hebrew people. Jacob's twelve sons became the founders of twelve tribes, and from the tribe of Judah came the names "Judea," "Jew," and "Judaism." After the captivity the name "Jew" was applied to all Israelites, and the name "Judaism" characterized their religion.

Early Judaism is distinguished for its monotheism, its code of laws, its temple and sacrificial system, its messianic hope, its judges, kings, and prophets, and its sacred Scriptures. It has one basic creed known as the *Shema*: "Hear, O Israel: The Lord our God is one Lord" (Deut. 6:4).

Judaism holds not only to its written law but to an oral law also. This, it claims, had its source in Moses the same as the written revelation. It has been passed down by word of mouth through the centuries. It was not written, in order that it might be distinguished from the basic law. Ultimately it began to be recorded and now forms what is known as the *Talmud*, composed of the *Mishna*, the Oral Law itself, and the *Gemara* or commentary. The Talmud and the Scriptures form the basis for Judaism.

Around the third century B.C. a Jewish sect known as the Chasidim (the pious or godly ones) arose. They opposed Hellenistic innovations and laid special stress on the ritual of purification and on separation. (Later the name was applied to a sect founded in Poland about the middle of the eighteenth century.) Instead of the Chasidim, two political parties soon appeared in the synagogue, known as the Pharisees (corresponding to the Hebrew *parush*, separated), and the Sadducees (from the Hebrew *Tsadduqim*, from *Tsadhoq*, the Hebrew form of Zadok, Solomon's High Priest). The Pharisees were noted for "strict and formal observation of rites and ceremonies of the written law and for insistence on the validity of the traditions of the elders." The Sadducees were "composed largely of the priestly aristocracy and [were] politically and doctrinally opposed to the Pharisees." There was also an ascetic order known as the Essenes and a political party known as the Herodians. Through the centuries there were other movements within Judaism, such as Karaism, which rejected Rabbinism and Talmudism and sought a return to the Scriptures, and Cabalism, which stressed a mystical interpretation of the Scriptures.

Today there are three principal groups in Judaism. Orthodox Judaism stresses the need of believing and living the written and oral law. Reform Judaism rejects the binding authority of the written and oral law and is known as Liberal or Progressive Judaism. Conservative Judaism differs from Orthodox Judaism mostly in external innovations such as occasional prayers in English, and from Reform Judaism as respects the Sabbath observance, the use of Hebrew, and the system of *Kashrus* (forbidden and permitted foods; permitted food is designated as *kasher*, more commonly spelled *kosher*).

CHRISTIANITY

The New Testament opens with the words, "The book of the generation of Jesus Christ, the son of David, the son of Abraham." Zacharias, the father of John the Baptist who was the forerunner of Christ, said: "Blessed be the Lord God of Israel; for he hath visited and redeemed his people. And hath raised up an horn of salvation for us in the house of his servant David" (Luke 1:68, 69). This is but a sample of the evidence that could be produced to show that Christianity did not appear upon the scene as a new religious faith. The Lord Jesus Christ himself stressed the fact that all things that were written in the Scriptures must be fulfilled. The Apostle Paul, whose writings form the major portion of the New Testament Epistles, said, "Now I say that Jesus Christ was a minister of the circumcision for the truth of God, to confirm the promises made unto the fathers" (Rom. 15:8). New Testament

Christianity is therefore neither a new faith nor a sectarian child of Judaism. It is Judaism in its truest form, the very fulfillment of the promises made to the fathers.

With the rejection of Jesus as the promised Messiah by the leaders of Israel and the continual rejection of the gospel of Christ as it was proclaimed in the synagogues through the ensuing years, the Christian faith soon became distinct and separate from Judaism. Being a missionary faith it spread rapidly among the Gentiles. The great number of Gentile adherents produced a problem regarding ritualism which resulted in the calling of a council at Jerusalem. At this council James, acting as spokesman, said, "Wherefore my sentence is, that we trouble not them, which from among the Gentiles are turned to God: but that we write unto them, that they abstain from pollutions of idols, and from fornication, and from things strangled, and from blood" (Acts 15: 19, 20).

As time went on the Gentile element grew while the Jewish element diminished, and the Christian faith developed towards the West rather than the East. The early centuries found it struggling for existence in the Roman Empire, but under Constantine it became the religion of Rome and ultimately of all of Europe. During the centuries after Constantine the organized Church found itself in a conflict for power between the churches at Rome and Constantinople. Finally, in the eleventh century, there was a complete break resulting in the Holy Catholic Church (Roman Catholic) and the Holy Orthodox Catholic and Apostolic Church (Greek Catholic).

In 1183 the Council at Verona excommunicated the Waldenses who became a separate Christian body. In 1457 a group of Bohemian Brethren broke from the Roman Church and became the Unitas Fratrum, known today as the Moravian Church. Then, early in the sixteenth century, came the Reformation which culminated in the formation of various "Protestant" denominations. Both Catholic and Protestant groups have had a strong missionary emphasis causing a world-wide diffusion of their respective forms of Christianity. In Catholicism the Church is the final authority and in Protestantism, the Bible.

HINDUISM

The name "Hindu" is derived from *Hind*, India, and represents "The native religious and social system of India. . . . Probably Hinduism is as old as, or older than, the Vedas . . . but as an organized historical system combining Aryan Vedic with indigenous Dravidian elements it takes form mainly in the last centuries before the Christian Era." (The Dravidians were the original dark-skinned aborigines who inhabited India, while the Aryans were a Caucasian people, "one branch of which early occupied the Iranian plateau, while another branch entered India, and conquered and amalgamated with the primitive inhabitants.")

The name *Veda* means "knowledge, sacred lore, sacred books" and applies to the most ancient sacred literature of the Hindus. The Vedic period is estimated to have begun about 1500 to 1000 B.C. The Vedas "display a vivid tendency to personify nature, and represent a stage of religion generally considered to be that of the Aryan invaders of India, but material from indigenous sources is embodied."

The heart of Hinduism is its caste system, of which there are four main historic castes into which a person is born, in which the hereditary occupation must be followed, and in which marriage and social relations must be maintained. From higher to lower these castes are: (1) the Brahmans, the priestly and intellectual caste; (2) the Kshatriyas, the governing and military caste; (3) the Vaisyas, the mercantile and agricultural caste; and (4) the Sudras, the artisan and laboring class. Within these four castes hundreds of subcastes have developed. "The native name for 'caste' (*varna*) signifies 'color' and the system seems to have originated in the endeavor of the light-hued Aryans to preserve their racial purity."

Early Hinduism, as seen in the Vedas, is mostly nature-worship consisting of prayers, chants, and sacred formulas. Between 1000 and 800 B.C. Priestly Hinduism developed, with a new type of literature known as the Brahmanas with particular stress placed upon sacrifices. From 800 to 600 B.C. Philosophic Hinduism arose, with a third set of sacred scriptures known as the *Upanishads*, and laying stress on the one Supreme Being or essence of the universe, the immaterial, impersonal, uncreated, infinite, indescribable supreme soul. About 250 B.C. Legalistic Hinduism took the ascendancy, with the Laws or Code of Manu as its basis, the stress being placed upon obedience to Law, especially the law of caste.

By the first century A.D. a Devotional Hinduism became popular and was based upon the Bhagavad-Gita (The Song of the Blessed One), a philosophical dialogue between the deity Krishna and prince Arjuna which gave to Hinduism new terms of devotion. Since that time a Popular Hinduism has developed, with its innumerable temples and shrines, its sacred places, seasons and festivals, its pilgrimages and ceremonial bathings, and its belief in transmigration.

ZOROASTRIANISM

Zoroastrianism is the ancient religion of Persia. It is named from its founder but is sometimes known as the Religion of the Parsees (from *Pars*—Persia). The actual date of Zoroaster is not known but has been conjecturally placed at 1000 B.C. (so Meyer and Duncker). Professor Jackson, in his comprehensive critical study, *Zoroaster, the Prophet of Ancient Iran,* places his date at 660 B.C. This date would bring its origin parallel to that of Shinto, but because of the uncertainty we shall place it first. If our placement were on the basis of adherents, it would come last, since it is said to have less than one-tenth of a million followers. It is generally considered a dying religion, but its relationship to the Bible makes it one of the most important for us to study. It was the Mohammedan invasion of Persia in 636, with its subsequent persecutions, that almost obliterated Zoroastrianism.

The new religion of Zoroaster was rooted in the old Aryan faith and reduced its polytheism to a dualism, "teaching that Ormazd, the lord of light and goodness, carries on a ceaseless war against Ahriman and the hosts of evil spirits who dwell in darkness. Ormadz created man to aid him, and eventually the good kingdom will be attained."

Zoroaster claimed that at the age of fifteen he was called into the presence of the deity Ahura Mazda (Ormazd) and appointed for the work of a prophet. During the following years he had seven further meetings with this deity. The result of his first ten years of preaching was only one convert. His success began with the conversion of the king, Vistaspa. His religion grew with the growth of Persia and the great empire under Darius. Greek writers from 480 to 330 B.C. show a lively interest in it. However, with the conquests of Alexander, and later the Parthians, Zoroastrianism went into a state of relapse and almost into polytheism. It was revived when Persia's independence was again established under Ardeshir I, an ardent Zoroastrian, and thrived during the years 226–651 A.D. When the Arabs conquered Persia they drove out, killed, or converted most of the Zoroastrians.

SHINTO

The proper name for this ancient religion of Japan is Shinto, not Shintoism. The Japanese *to* is the equivalent of our *ism;* the use of both is duplication. *Shinto* means "the way of the gods." Although the oldest scripture of Shinto, the *Ko-ji-ki* ("Records of Ancient Matters"), was only completed in 712 A.D., it records the traditional myths of creation and then deals with the history of the Japanese Imperial Line from the accession of the first Mikado, Jimmu Tenno, in 660 B.C., to the reign of the Empress Suiko in 628 A.D.

Webster describes Shinto as "The ethnic cult and religion of the Japanese, consisting chiefly in the reverence shown to the spirits of imperial ancestors and historical personages, and to some deities of nature. Inherent in the race, Shinto was long influenced by and interwoven with Buddhism until the two were separated by law after 1871. The cult as embodied in the temples is not regarded as a religion . . . and is distinguished from the religious sects also called *Shinto,* which have been founded by private persons by building tenets on some phases of the Shinto tradition." Shinto is classified by many Japanese, European, and American authorities as a patriotic cult rather than a religion. Nevertheless, there is a definite religious element present.

Originally the religion of Shinto was only nature worship. Then the divine origin of the first Mikado was taught as being one of direct lineal descent from the Sun-goddess. This brought emperor-worship into Shinto. Shinto shrines were built everywhere and maintained by the government. Worship in these shrines has always been individual rather than congregational. Shinto has no definite theological creed nor ethical code and seems to find its fulfillment in subservience to the Mikado.

After the military defeat of 1945, Emperor Hirohito told his people, "The ties between Us and Our people . . . are not predicated on the false conception that the Emperor is divine, and that the Japanese people are superior to other races, and are fated to rule the world. The Tenno (Emperor) is not a living God." This would seem to have been the death blow to Shinto. It is wrong, however, to think of Shinto as primarily emperor- and empress-worship. The worship of a mythological god or goddess had not been discontinued. War heroes, statesmen, and even a scholar were also enshrined. In what is known as the Family Cult there is ancestor worship.

The strongest religious development in Shinto took place with the arrival of the Buddhist missionaries from China in 552 A.D. An amalgamation of the two faiths began to be effected. Taoism and Confucianism also found fertile soil here. The revival of Shinto—beginning in the eighteenth century under Kada and his pupil Mabuchi, enhanced by the commentary of Motoori on the *Ko-ji-ki* and the writings of Hirata—culminated in the Restoration of 1868 and the following law of separation, but it did not utterly uproot the religious influences of these faiths. Shinto shrines were divested of Buddhist images, scriptures, and decorations, and Shinto became a State Religion. The development of sects soon began. There are three known as Pure Shinto Sects, two Confucian Sects, the Mountain Sects, two Purification Sects, and three Faith-healing Sects. So, in spite of the results of the war and the destruction of the State Shrines, Shinto continues in Japan.

TAOISM

The three officially recognized religions of China, known as the *San Chiao*, are Taoism, Confucianism, and Buddhism. Unlike the other two, Taoism was not named after its founder Lao-tze. *Tao* means "way" and referred originally to the way of the heavens revolving about the earth and causing certain phenomena on the earth. At first the Tao was believed to be located at the celestial pole as the seat of power, because all revolved about it, but later the Tao was taken as the universal cosmic energy or impersonal being behind nature, producing the *yin* and the *yang*, the negative and the positive principles of nature. Taoism was therefore basically a philosophical system.

Lao-tze was born 604 B.C. in Honan Province, Central China. He was a contemporary of Confucius, although about fifty years his senior, and also of Zoroaster in Persia, of Mahavira and Buddha in India, and of Isaiah, Jeremiah and Ezekiel in Palestine. He was both a philosopher and public official. During the Chou dynasty he was court archivist. He is accredited with having written most of the *Tao Teh King* ("The Way of Reason and Virtue"). The designation used for God in the sacred books of the East, *Ti* (Ruler), occurs only once in this work.

Lao-tze never claimed divinity for himself, but in 156 A.D. sacrifices were ordered to be offered to him. In the first century A.D. a Chinese scholar named Chang Tao-ling became what has been called the first pope of Taoism. All his life he studied alchemy and magic and corrupted Taoism with it.

Taoism flourished only during those few times that the Chinese emperors were favorable to it. It was in constant opposition to Confucianism and later to Buddhism. The claim of some of its doctors to cure disease by magic brought it into conflict with the government, which often resulted in official condemnation. Such, for example, took place in 825–827 A.D. when the Emperor Pao-Li banished all Taoist doctors to the two southernmost provinces of China. In 1661–1721 Emperor Kang Hsi endeavored to suppress Taoism and its various sects. Had he succeeded, the Boxer Uprising of 1900 would never have occurred, since it originated with an ardent Taoist sect whose adherents believed that they were immune to the bullets of foreigners, basing their faith on the statement in the Tao Teh King that "When coming among soldiers, he need not fear arms and weapons."

The significance of *Tao* developed from the primary idea of "way" or "order" of the moral and physical world to its highest technical application to the Supreme Being, the philosophic Absolute. But the ethical idealism of its founder has been forsaken and Taoism has become a conglomeration of animism, polytheism, and occultism. It is unfortunate, in view of all this, that the word *Tao* was used in the Chinese Gospel of John to translate the word *logos* in the passage "In the beginning was the *Tao*, and the *Tao* was with God, and the *Tao* was God."

JAINISM

What was destined to become the Jaina religion began as a reform movement within Hinduism. Vardhamana Jnatiputra was born in 599 B.C. in Vesali, a town of northeast India. He was a Hindu of the second class since his father was a petty rajah. He was reared in luxury and married into another princely family. After the death of his parents he renounced everything and became a religious ascetic in the best Hindu tradition. This he determined to be for twelve years. For thirteen months he wore clothes and then went naked for the rest of the time, indifferent alike to the smell of filth and of sandalwood. For these twelve years he meditated upon himself; and in the thirteenth year, in the midst of abstract meditation, he is said to have reached Nirvana, the complete and full, the unobstructed, infinite Absolute. He then left asceticism to become a leader and teacher, winning large numbers of converts and propagating his particular form of religion which, strangely enough, was that one should worship no man or object and simply live a quiet, harmless life.

Mahavira (Great Hero), as his followers called him, soon came to be worshipped by them. He was considered to be the last of a line of saints or conquerors called *jinas*. "Mahavira and his 23 supposed predecessors are called *jinas* (conquerors), *tirhankaras* (ford-finders), and *kevalins* (single ones)" (*Webster*). His followers called themselves *Jaina*, "Followers of the Jina." The sacred scriptures of

Jainism portray him as sinless, omniscient, pre-existent, and descended from heaven.

The two main sects of Jainism developed out of a dispute over the wearing of clothes. During a famine in north India about 310 B.C., some 12,000 Jains emigrated to south India. There the warmer climate allowed a fuller asceticism which included the discarding of clothes. By around 82 A.D. this difference in the two groups caused a complete break. Those of the north were called the *Svetambara*, the Sanskrit for "clad in white," and those of the south were called the *Digambara*, the "sky-clad." This difference was carried even to their idols, the one sect clothing theirs and the other one not. When the Mohammedans invaded India they compelled the Digambara to wear loin-cloths.

Many other sects also developed, the Svetambara Jains dividing into more than 80. Important among these was the Sthanakvasi sect which rejected idol worship and maintained that only 33 of the scriptures called the *Agamas* ("Precepts") were sacred. The Svetambara sect recognizes 45, while another one holds to some 84.

The Jains are especially noted for their architecture. Travelers from all parts of the world have visited their temples at Kaligamalai, Ahmedabad, Ellora, Ajmere, and Mount Abu. The Jain *stupa* (memorial mount) at Mathura is probably the oldest building in India. The Jains are today a diminishing group, but will always remain historically important to India.

BUDDHISM

Prince Siddhartha was born in India around 560 B.C. The exact date is uncertain. His father was chief of the Sakyas, and so he came to be called Sakyamuni (also Shakya Muni), Sage of the Sakyas. The warrior caste into which he was born claimed to belong to the Gautama clan and so he was popularly called Gautama. He was reared in excessive luxury, married at nineteen, and had his first son at twenty-nine. At this time he wearied of his luxury, became very distressed over thoughts of old age, sickness and death, and, in true Hindu fashion, sought "salvation" in renunciation and meditation. He therefore left his wife, his newborn son, and his father's inheritance. For six years, first through philosophic speculation and then bodily asceticism, he tried to win peace. At 35, while meditating one night under a pipal tree (the sacred Bo tree), he received enlightenment. It is this occasion that caused him to be given the title *Buddha,* Enlightened One. He is generally referred to as Gautama Buddha.

His enlightenment consisted in the apprehension of "four noble truths," listed by *Webster* as follows: "(1) that all life is subject to suffering; (2) that desire or the will to live is the cause of repeated existences in which sorrow is inevitable; (3) that only the annihilation of desire (that is, yearning, craving, ambition, as distinct from will) can give release; (4) that the way of escape is the 'Eightfold Path' of right belief, right resolve, right word, right act, right life, right effort, right thinking, right meditation."

This godless doctrine of salvation from repeated transmigrations Gautama immediately began to preach throughout his native country of Magadha in north India. We say "godless" because it was exactly that, for Gautama taught that it could be attained without any of the conventions of religion such as worship, ceremony, dogma, priesthood, or even belief in a deity. Buddhism therefore, in its early form, was not a religion.

Gautama Buddha taught for 45 years up and down the Ganges valley, winning converts, establishing an order of wandering monks, and building up his teachings into the faith now known as Buddhism. "Buddha denied the special virtue of caste, ritualism, and asceticism, and insisted upon the necessity of pity, kindness, and patience, for salvation."

It is basic in the nature of man to believe in deity, but Buddha offered no such faith. Buddhism in southern Asia endeavored to be true to the teachings of its founder and became known as *Hinayana* Buddhism (The Lesser Vehicle), also as *Therevada* (Southern) Buddhism. In northern Asia Buddha was deified, and this branch became known as the *Mahayana* (The Greater Vehicle). Buddhism spread under the influence of its missionaries to the neighboring countries of Ceylon, Tibet, Burma, and Siam, and as far away as China and Japan. But in India, about a thousand years after its inception, Buddhism became torn by petty wrangling (such as the size and cut of their robes) and faded away under the force of the Islamic invasion. It has flourished mostly in China and Japan.

CONFUCIANISM

The correct Chinese name for Confucianism is *Yu-Kiao,* "the System of the Learned."

Kung Fu-tse (literally "Philosopher Kung," also written K'ung Fu-tzu and Latinized to Confucius) lived from 551 to 479 B.C. He was born in the state of Lu, now the province of Shantung, China. He was the youngest of 11 children. His father died when he was three. He married at 19 and had one son besides several daughters. Even before his marriage he began to devote himself to the study of ancient writings, and at about 21 began a school which ultimately numbered 3000. Here he taught history, literature, music, natural science, and government. He became chief magistrate of his town and advanced until he became prime minister of Lu. This position he resigned and taught from state to state for some 12 or 13 years. "Not a religious teacher, his precepts (*Confucianism*) dealt with morals, the family system, social reforms, statecraft; his maxims, still taught as a guide for daily life of people, are of practical value as a utilitarian philosophy; called himself 'a transmitter, not an originator'; his writings consisted chiefly of comments on the Chinese classics; has had many disciples who added much to Confucian literature. The *Analects*, a brief record of his teachings on various subjects, is one of the Four Books of Chinese Classics" (*Webster's Biographical Dictionary*).

The veneration of Confucius began with the high esteem in which his disciples held him. In

195 B.C. the Emperor of China offered an animal sacrifice at his tomb. By 57 A.D. regular sacrifice to him was ordered at the imperial and provincial colleges until, by 555 A.D., separate temples for his worship were erected. In 1906 an Imperial Rescript gave him the rank of "Co-assessor with the deities Heaven and Earth." Yuan Shi Kai, the first President of the Republic of China, continued the worship of Confucius.

ISLAM

Islam is frequently and erroneously called Mohammedanism (or Muhammedanism), which is defined by *Webster* as "The religion, doctrines, or precepts, of Mohammed; called by believers *Islam.*" *Islam* is the infinitive of *aslama* and means "to submit." The present participle of this Arabic verb is *muslim* and this gives us the name "Moslem" (or Muslim). An adherent of this faith does not refer to himself as a Mohammedan but a Muslim, a "submitting one."

Mohammed (Arabic, *Muhammad,* "praiseworthy, highly praised") was born at Mecca, Arabia, in 570 A.D. He was left an orphan and was reared by his uncle Abu-Talib. From shepherd boy he turned to camel driver and then merchant. He married Khadija, a wealthy widow, in 595. *Webster* summarizes what followed in these words: "...was disturbed about low condition of Arabs, their superstition and ignorance; after years of meditation, felt (c. 610) that he had a call as prophet and teacher for his race;

for a few years, taught the new religion in secret at Mecca, converting his wife, his cousin and adopted son Ali, his friend Abu-Bakr, and a small number of proselytes; first taught openly (c. 613); followers persecuted by Meccan leaders and himself strongly opposed because of his struggle against ancient tribal and religious customs; sought refuge in Taif (c. 620); with loyal followers, fled from Mecca to Yathrib (modern Medina), arriving Sept. 20, 622; Arabic year of the flight (*hegira*) later used to mark beginning of Mohammedan era; enthusiastically received; sought to attain public security at Medina; waged civil war against Meccans, finally successful (620–627); established principles of Islam, embodied in the Koran; returned to Mecca as master (629); publicly recognized as chief and prophet (630); extended power to include all Arabia (630–632); died at Medina. After death of Khadija (620), married several wives . . . who had great influence over him" (*Biographical Dictionary*).

It was at Medina that Mohammed set up the rule of Allah with himself as dictator, building a mosque for daily prayer, engaging in many military campaigns, changing the "facing" (*qiblah*) of prayer from Jerusalem to Mecca, and endeavoring to bring Judaism and Christianity into complete dependence upon him. After his death the movement was under the leadership for 28 years of caliphs, first Abu Bakr, then Omar, Othman, and finally Ali, after whose assassination Islam broke up into various sects, each warring against the other. Today there are about 72 of these.

In a number of passages of the Koran Mohammed is closely associated with Allah, so that obedience to the Prophet is part of submission to God. Much later on he was exalted in the minds of many to a place of sinlessness and as mediator for the faithful on the Last Day. Although he himself disclaimed working miracles, Mirkhond wrote in the fifteenth century a life of Mohammed including some fifty pages of miracles he was supposed to have performed.

SIKHISM

Nanak was born in 1469 A.D. in the province of Punjab, India. His father was a second caste Hindu employed by a Moslem feudal lord. As a boy of seven he is said to have told his Hindu teacher that the way to know God—whom he called *Sat Nam,* that is, "True Name"—is by His mercy, rather than to study the Vedas. It was probably thus early in in life that his Hindu background and the influence of at least a partial Islamic environment were laying the foundation for the later attempt he made to harmonize Hinduism and Islam, only to produce a new religion known as Sikhism.

Because of a strong dislike for physical activity and a preference for meditation, Nanak was thought to be a disgrace to his family. Even when he had a government position with his brother-in-law, he remained deeply unhappy. During one period he left his wife and children and retired to the desert. On another occasion he disappeared into a forest where he claimed he was taken in a vision to God's presence.

Among other things, he was told, "My Name is God, the primal Brahma. And thou art the divine Guru." *Guru* means "teacher, venerable one."

After this experience Nanak took the attire of a religious ascetic, wearing only a loin-cloth, and began his proclamation, "There is no Hindu and no Musalman [Moslem]!" He took with him on his missionary journeys a Moslem named Mardana who was a musician. Singing and preaching, they traveled widely, visiting many sacred places of Hinduism. He compiled part of the sacred scriptures of the Sikhs (*Sikh* is the Hindu for "disciple"), which later became known as the *Granth* ("Book"). His teaching was strongly monotheistic.

Within 60 years after his death in 1538, he was deified by his followers. Gurdas 13:25 says, "Guru Nanak is God, the Supreme Brahma." After the death of the tenth Guru in 1708, changes took place in Sikhism, and loyalty shifted from the personal Guru to the Granth, and it is the Granth that is worshipped today, practically as an idol. It is called *Granth Saheb* ("Lord Book") and a copy occupies a throne under a jewelled canopy at Amritsar in the central shrine of Sikhism. Sikhism today has some four million adherents, most of them living in Punjab, their original ancestral home.

Chapter Two

Sacred Literature

The importance of the written word is evident from the fact that only those religions have survived which had some authoritative writings as the basis of their faith and practice. Most of these writings have been translated into English and may be found in many libraries. Since not all students have access to these, we shall select quotations from the various books under their respective religious headings to enable the reader to get a bit of the inner feelings of each of these religions. This selection is necessarily limited and cannot include even one quotation from each of the many books of some of these religions. It must also be remembered that in practically all of these religions there are writings not listed as sacred literature which nonetheless have strong authority and help to formulate both the ceremonial and creedal aspects of these faiths.

JUDAISM

The sacred books of Judaism are contained in the *Torah She-Bi-Khetab,* the Written Law. This contains the same thirty-nine books as the Old Testament of the Christian Bible but in a different order, arranged in three groupings known as the *Torah* (the Law), the *Nebiim* (the Prophets), and the *Kethubim* (the Writings). The first five, *Bereshit* (Genesis), *Shemot* (Exodus), *Vayikra* (Leviticus), *Bamidbar* (Numbers), and *Debarim* (Deuteronomy), are generally conceded more authority than the rest.

In addition to this there is the *Torah She-Be-Al Peh,* the Oral Law. Like the Written Law, this is supposed to have had its source in Moses. It actually originated much later, and was passed down by word of mouth through the centuries until it was gradually reduced to writing, from about 220 to 500 A.D., and is now found in what is known as the *Talmud.* There are some who may not consider the Talmud as part of Israel's sacred literature, but the *Encyclopedia of Jewish Knowledge* gives the following statement made by Rabbi Maurice J. Bloom: "During the centuries after its completion, the Talmud became an authoritative source for Judaism, second only to the Torah itself, and in some cases, indeed, rivalling the Torah in importance."

Since everyone has access to the Bible, we shall give here certain selections from the Talmud. But first, for the benefit of those not too well acquainted with the Talmud, let us give the following summary from *Webster's New International Dictionary*: "The body of Jewish civil and canonical law, consisting of the combined Mishna or text, and Gemara, or commentary; also, restrictedly, the Gemara alone. There are two Talmuds, named from the region in which they originated, the *Palestinian* . . . and the *Babylonian*. . . . They contain the same Mishna, but different Gemaras. The Palestinian was practically completed in the 4th century, and the Babylonian in the 5th or 6th century A.D. The latter is about three times as large as the former, and practically superseded it as an authority."

The Talmud

(The Messianic hope has always held an important place and still does in Orthodox circles today. We have therefore selected the following Messianic references from the tract *Sanhedrin*.)

Mishnah. All Israel have a portion in the world to come, for it is written, "Thy people are all righteous; they shall inherit the land forever, the branch of my planting, the work of my hands, that I may be glorified." But the following have no portion therein: he who maintains that resurrection is not a Biblical doctrine, the Torah was not divinely revealed, and an Epikoros [Epicurean or licentious person]. R. [Rabbi] Akiba added: One who reads uncanonical books. Also one who whispers (a charm) over a wound and says, "I will bring none of these diseases upon thee which I brought upon the Egyptians: for I am the Lord that healeth thee." Abba Saul says: Also one who pronounces the divine name as it is spelt. . . (90a).

Gemara. And why such (severity)?—A Tanna taught: Since he denied the resurrection of the dead, therefore he shall not share in that resurrection, for in all the measures (of punishment or reward) taken by the Holy One, blessed be He, the Divine act befits the (human) deed....

R. Hisda opposed (two verses). It is written, *Then the moon shall be confounded, and the sun ashamed, when the Lord of Hosts shall reign,* whilst (elsewhere) it is written, *Moreover the light of the moon shall be as the light of the sun, and the light of the sun shall be sevenfold, as the light of seven days.*—It is no difficulty: the latter refers to the Messianic era, the former to the world to come. And according to Samuel, who maintained, This world differs from the Messianic era only in respect of the servitude of the Diaspora, it is still no difficulty: the latter refers to the camp of the righteous, the former to the camp of the Divine Presence (91b).

It has been taught: R. Meir said, Whence do we know resurrection from the Torah? From the verse, *Then shall Moses and the children of Israel sing this song unto the Lord*: not *sang* but *shall sing* is written: thus resurrection is taught in the Torah. Likewise thou readest, *Then shall Joshua build an altar unto the Lord God of Israel*: not *built,* but *shall build* is written: thus resurrection is intimated in the Torah. If so, *Then did Solomon build an high place for Chemosh, the abomination of Moab*: does that too mean that he *shall* build? But (there) the Writ regards him as though he had built.

R. Joshua b. Levi said: Whence is resurrection

derived from the Torah? From the verse, *Blessed are they that dwell in thy house: they shall ever praise thee. Selah.* Not *praised thee,* but *shall praise thee* is stated: thus resurrection is taught in the Torah . . . (91b).

Our Rabbis taught: In the seven year cycle at the end of which the son of David will come—in the first year, this verse will be fulfilled: *And I will cause it to rain upon one city and cause it not to rain upon another city;* in the second, the arrows of hunger will be sent forth; in the third, a great famine, in the course of which men, women, and children, pious men and saints will die, and the Torah will be forgotten by its students; in the fourth, partial plenty; in the fifth, great plenty, when men will eat, drink and rejoice, and the Torah will return to its disciples; in the sixth, (Heavenly) sounds; in the seventh, wars; and at the conclusion of the septannate the son of David will come. . . (Footnote on the sixth: Either Heavenly voices announcing the advent of Messiah, or the blast of the great Shofar; cf. Isa. XXVII, 13.) (97a).

It has been taught: R. Nehorai said: In the generation when Messiah comes, young men will insult the old, and old men will stand before the young (to give them honor); daughters will rise up against their mothers, and daughters-in-law against their mothers-in-law. The people shall be dog-faced, and a son will not be abashed in his father's presence (97a).

R. Hama b. Hanina said: The son of David will not come until even the pettiest kingdom ceases (to have power) over Israel, as it is written, *He shall both cut off the sprigs with pruning hooks, and take away and cut down the branches;* and this is followed by, *In that time shall the present be brought unto the Lord of hosts of a people that is scattered and peeled.*

Ze'iri said in R. Hanina's name: The son of David will not come until there are no conceited men in Israel, as it is written, *For then I will take away out of the midst of thee them that rejoice in thy pride;* which is followed by, *I will also leave in the midst of thee an afflicted and poor people, and they shall take refuge in the name of the Lord. . . .*

R. Johanan said: When you see a generation ever dwindling, hope for him (the Messiah), as it is written, *And the afflicted people thou wilt save.* R. Johanan said: When thou seest a generation overwhelmed by many troubles as by a river, await him, as it is written, *When the enemy shall come in like a flood, the Spirit of the Lord shall lift up a standard against him;* which is followed by, *And the Redeemer shall come to Zion.*

R. Alexandri said: R. Joshua b. Levi pointed out a contradiction. It is written, *in its time* (will the Messiah come), whilst it is also written, *I (the Lord) will hasten it!*—If they are worthy, I will hasten it: if not, (he will come) at the due time. R. Alexandri said: R. Joshua opposed two verses: it is written, *And behold, one like the son of man came with the clouds of heaven;* whilst (elsewhere) it is written, *(Behold, thy king cometh unto thee. . .) lowly, and riding upon an ass!*—If they are meritorious, (he will come) *with the clouds of heaven;* if not, *lowly and riding upon an ass* (98a).

R. Hiyya b. Abba said in R. Johanan's name: All the prophets prophesied (all the good things) only in respect of the Messianic era; but as for the world to come, *the eye hath not seen, O Lord, beside thee, what he hath prepared for them that waiteth for him.* Now, he disagrees with Samuel, who said: This world differs from (that of) the days of the Messiah only in respect of servitude to (foreign) powers (99a).

CHRISTIANITY

The sacred book of Christianity is called the *Bible.* This is divided into the Old Testament and the New Testament. The former contains the same books as the Jewish Bible but in the order in which they are found in the *Septuagint,* the Greek translation made around 250 B.C. The name is derived from the Latin *septuaginta* (seventy), with reference to the seventy scholars who translated it. A group of books known as the *Apocrypha* (hidden, secret) is included in the Roman Catholic canon of the Old Testament as follows: Tobias, Judith, additions to Esther, the Book of Wisdom, Ecclesiasticus, Baruch (of which chapter six is the epistle of Jeremias), the Song of the Three Holy Children (67 verses following Daniel 3:23), the History of Susanna (a chapter 13 of Daniel), Bel and the Dragon (a chapter 14 of Daniel), I Maccabees, and II Maccabees. The twenty-seven books of the New Testament are the same in both the Catholic and Protestant canons.

The readings for this section have been selected as follows: From the Old Testament, our own translation of the twenty-third Psalm from the Septuagint, keeping it as literal as possible in order to give the feeling of the Greek original; from the Apocrypha, an interesting section regarding Jeremias' hiding the ark at the time of the captivity; and from the New Testament, two selections from the ancient translations.

The Septuagint

Psalm 23

(The) Lord shepherds me, and he lets me want nothing.

Into a place of young verdure, there he encamped me: upon (the) water of rest he has nourished me.

My soul he has restored: he has guided me upon the beaten paths of righteousness, for the sake of his name.

For even if I should go in (the) midst of (the) shadow of death, I shall not be afraid of evils, because *thou* art with *me;* thy rod and thy staff, these have comforted me.

Thou hast prepared before me a table in (the) presence of the ones afflicting me: thou hast anointed in oil my head, and thy wine-cup inebriates as (the) strongest.

Also thy mercy follows me close all the days of my life, and my dwelling (shall be) in (the) house of (the) Lord into far distant days.

The Apocrypha

II Maccabees 2: 1–8

1 Now it is found in the descriptions of Jeremias
the prophet, that he commanded them that went
into captivity, to take the fire, as it hath been signi-
fied, and how he gave charge to them that were carried away into captivity.
2 And how he gave them the law that they should
not forget the commandments of the Lord, and that
they should not err in their minds, seeing the idols
of gold, and silver, and the ornaments of them.
3 And with other such like speeches, he exhorted
them that they would not remove the law from
their heart.
4 It was also contained in the same writing, how
the prophet, being warned by God, commanded that
the tabernacle and the ark should accompany him,
till he came forth to the mountain where Moses went
up, and saw the inheritance of God.
5 And when Jeremias came thither he found a
hollow cave: and he carried in thither the tabernacle,
and the ark, and the altar of incense, and so stopped
the door.
6 Then some of them that followed him came
up to mark the place: but they could not find it.
7 And when Jeremias perceived it, he blamed
them, saying: The place shall be unknown, till God
gather together the congregation of the people, and
receive them to mercy.
8 And then the Lord will show these things, and
the majesty of the Lord shall appear, and there shall

be a cloud as it was also shewed to Moses, and he shewed it when Solomon prayed that the place might be sanctified to the great God.

The New Testament

John 1: 1–14

(Wiclif—1380 A.D.)

IN the bigynnynge was the word and the word was at god, and god was the word, this was in the bigynnynge at god, alle thingis weren made bi hym: and withouten hym was made no thing. that thing that was made in him was liif, and the liif was the lizt of men, and the liz schyneth in derkness: and derknessis comprehendiden not it.

A man was sente fro god to whom the name was Ion, this man cam in to witnessynge, that he schulde bere witnessynge of the lizt, that alle men schulden bileve bi hym, he was not the lizt: but that he schulde bere witnessynge of the lizt, ther was a verri lizt: whiche liztneth eche man that cometh into this world, he was in the world, and the world was made bi hym: and the world knewe hym not, he cam in to his owne thingis: hise resceyueden hym not: but hou many euer resceiueden hym: he zaf to hem power to be made the sones of god, to hem that bileueden in his name, the whiche not of blodis nether of the wille of fleisch, nether of the wille of man: but ben borun of god, and the word was made man: and dwellide among us, and we han seen the glorie of hym: as the glorie of the oon bigetun sone of the fadir, ful of grace and of truthe.

ROMANS 11:25–28

(Tyndale—1534 A.D.)

I wolde not that this secrete shuld be hyd from you my brethren (lest ye shud be wyse in youre awne consaytes) that partly blyndnes is happened in Israel, vntyll the fulnes of the gentyls be come in: and so all Israel shal be saved. As it is written: There shall come oute of Sion he that doth delyver, and shall turn awaye the vngodlynes of Iacob. And this is my covenant vnto them, when I shall take awaye their synnes. As concernynge the gospell, they are enemies for youre sakes: but as touchinge the election they are loved for the fathers sakes.

HINDUISM

The most ancient books of Hinduism are the four *Vedas*—"the *Rig-Veda,* the oldest and most important, comprising more than a thousand hymns; the *Yajur-Veda,* comprising liturgical and ritualistic formulae in verse and prose; the *Sama-Veda,* hymns, many of which occur in the Rig-Veda, for which musical notation is added or indicated; and the *Atharva-Veda,* in verse and prose, comprising charms, prayers, curses, spells, etc., as well as some theosophic and cosmogonic hymns, and written in a cruder and more popular style than the preceding." Our first group of quotations is taken from the Rig-Veda.

This will be followed by a quotation from the *Upanishads* of Philosophic Hinduism and then by one from the *Bhagavad-Gita* of Devotional Hinduism.

The Rig-Veda

TO AGNI

Great Agni, though thine essence be but one,
Thy forms are three; as fire thou blazest here,
As lightning flashest in the atmosphere,
In heaven thou flamest as the golden sun.

It was in heaven thou hadst thy primal birth,
But thence of yore a holy sage benign,
Conveyed thee down on human hearths to shine,
And thou abid'st a denizen of earth.

TO VARUNA

1. This laud of the self-radiant wise Aditya shall be supreme o'er all that is in greatness.
   I beg renown of Varuna the mighty, the god exceeding kind to him who worships.
2. Having extolled thee, Varuna, with thoughtful care may we have high fortune in thy service.
   Singing thy praises like the fires at coming, day after day, of mornings rich in cattle.
3. May we be in thy keeping, O thou leader, wide ruling Varuna, Lord of many heroes.
   O sons of Aditi, forever faithful, pardon us, gods, admit us to your friendship.

Sacred Literature

To Indra

Thou, Indra, oft of old hast quaffed
With keen delight, our Soma draught.
All gods delicious Soma love;
But thou, all other gods above.
Thy mother knew how well this juice
Was fitted for her infant's use,
Into a cup she crushed the sap
Which thou didst sip upon her lap;
Yes, Indra, on thy natal morn,
The very hour that thou wast born,
Thou didst those jovial tastes display,
Which still survive in strength today.

The Upanishads

Second Adhyaya

First Brahmana

1. There was formerly the proud Gargya Balaki, a man of great reading. He said to Ajatasatru of Kasi, "Shall I tell you Brahman?" Ajatasatru said: "We give a thousand (cows) for that speech (of yours), for verily all people run away, saying, Janaka (the King of Mithila) is our father (patron)."

2. Gargya said: "The person that is in the sun, that I adore as Brahman." Ajatasatru said to him: "No, no! Do not speak to me on this. I adore him verily as supreme, the head of all beings, the king. Whoso adores him thus, becomes supreme, the head of all beings, a king."

3. Gargya said: "The person that is in the moon (and in the mind), that I adore as Brahman." Ajatasatru said to him: "No, no! Do not speak to me on this. I adore him verily as the great, clad in white raiment, as Soma, the king. Whoso adores him thus, Soma is poured out and poured forth for him day by day, and his food does not fail."

4. Gargya said: "The person that is in the lightning (and in the heart), that I adore as Brahman." Ajatasatru said to him: "No, no! Do not speak to me on this. I adore him verily as the luminous. Whoso adores him thus, becomes luminous, and his offspring becomes luminous."

5. . . . The person that is in the ether . . . I adore him as what is full, and quiescent . . . .

6. . . . The person that is in the wind . . . I adore him as Indra Vaikuntha, as the unconquerable arm (of Maruts) . . . .

7. . . . The person that is in the fire . . . I adore him as powerful. . . .

8. . . . The person that is in the water . . . I adore him as likeness. . . .

9. . . . The person that is in the mirror . . . I adore him verily as the brilliant. . . , etc.

The Svetasvatara Upanishad

Fourth Adhyaya

8. He who does not know that indestructible being of the Rig-Veda, that highest ether-like (Self) wherein all the gods reside, of what use is the

Rig-Veda to him? Those only who know it, rest contented.

9. That from which the maker (mayin) sends forth all this—the sacred verses, the offerings, the sacrifices, the panaceas, the past, the future, and all that the Vedas declared—in that the other is bound up through that art (maya).

10. Know that Prakriti (nature) is Maya (art), and the great Lord the Mayin (maker); the whole world is filled with what are his members.

11. If a man has discerned him, who, being one only, rules over every germ (cause), in whom all this comes together and comes asunder again, who is the lord, the bestower of blessing, the adorable god, then he passes forever into that peace.

12. He, the creator and supporter of the gods, Rudra, the great seer, the lord of all, who saw Hiranyagarbha being born, may he endow us with good thoughts.

13. He who is the sovereign of the gods, he in whom all the worlds rest, he who rules over all two-footed and four-footed beings, to that god let us sacrifice an oblation.

14. He who has known him who is more subtile than subtile, in the midst of chaos, creating all things, having many forms, alone enveloping everything, the happy one (Siva), passes into peace for ever.

15. He also was in time the guardian of this world, the lord of all, hidden in all beings. In him the Brahmarhis and the deities are united, and he who knows him cuts the fetters of death asunder.

16. He who knows Siva (the blessed) hidden in all

beings, like the subtile film that arises from out the clarified butter, alone enveloping everything—he who knows the god, is freed from all fetters.

17. That god, the maker of all things, the great Self, always dwelling in the heart of man, is perceived by the heart, the soul, the mind; they who know it become immortal.

18. When the light has risen, there is no day, no night, neither existence nor non-existence; Siva (the blessed) alone is there. That is the eternal, the adorable light of Savitri—and the ancient wisdom proceeded thence.

19. No one has grasped him above, or across, or in the middle. There is no image of him whose name is Great Glory.

20. His form cannot be seen, no one perceives him with the eye. Those who through heart and mind know him thus abiding in the heart, become immortal.

The Bhagavad-Gita

Lesson the Second

ARJUNA SPAKE:

54. "What are the words for the man of abiding wisdom who stays in concent, O long-haired one? What will the man of abiding wisdom say? How shall he sit or walk?"

THE LORD SPAKE:

55. "When one leaves all the loves that dwell in the mind, O son of Pritha, and is gladdened only in

his Self by his Self, then he is said to be of abiding wisdom.

56. He whose mind is undismayed in pain, who is freed from longings for pleasure, from whom passion, fear, and wrath have fled, is called a man of abiding prudence, a saintly man.

57. He who is without affection for aught, and whatever fair or foul fortune may betide neither rejoices in it nor loathes it, has wisdom abidingly set.

58. When such a one draws his sense-instruments altogether from the objects of the sense-instruments, as a tortoise draws in its limbs, he has wisdom abidingly set.

59. The ranges of sense vanish away from a body-dweller who haunts them not, save only relish; and at sight of the Supreme the relish likewise passes away from him.

60. For though the prudent man strive, O son of Kunti, his forward instruments of sense carry away his mind perforce.

61. Let him hold all these in constraint and sit under the Rule, given over to me; for he who has his sense-instruments under his sway has wisdom abidingly set."

Lesson the Sixth

ARJUNA SPAKE:

37. "If one possessed of faith mortify himself not, and his mind swerve from the Rule, so that he wins not to accomplishment of the Rule, into what ways comes he, O Krishna?

38. Falls he not from both paths, and perishes he not like a riven cloud, O mighty-armed one, unestablished and bewildered in the road to Brahma?

39. This is my doubt, O Krishna, it is meet for thee to resolve altogether; there is no resolver of this doubt beside thee."

THE LORD SPAKE:

40. "Son of Pritha, neither here nor in the other world is there destruction for him; for none that does righteousness, beloved, comes to evil estate.

41. He that is fallen from the Rule wins to the worlds of them that do godly deeds, and dwells there changeless years; then he is born in the house of poor and prosperous folks.

42. Or haply he may be born in the race of wise men of the Rule; but such birth as this is very hard to win in the world.

43. There he is given that rule of the understanding which he had in his former body, O child of Kurus, and therefore he strives further for adeptship.

44. For he is led onward, without will of his own, by that former striving; if he have even the wish to know the Rule, he passes beyond the Word-Brahma.

45. But the man of the Rule who labours stoutly, when cleansed of defilements and brought to adeptship through many births, goes thence by the way supreme.

46. Greater than mortifiers of the flesh is deemed

the man of the Rule, greater also than men of knowledge, and greater than doers of works; therefore be thou a man of the Rule, O Arjuna.

47. Of all men of the Rule I deem him who worships me in faith with his inward Self dwelling in me to be most utterly *under the Rule.*"

Lesson the Seventh

THE LORD SPAKE:

1. "Hear, son of Pritha, how, if thou labourest upon the Rule with mind clinging to me and with me for thy dwelling-place, thou shalt surely know me in my fulness.

2. I will tell thee of the knowledge and discernment which if thou possessest there shall remain naught else to know.

3. Of thousands of men, but few strive for adeptship; of the adepts that strive, but few know me in verity.

4. A nature have I of eight orders—Earth, Water, Fire, Wind, Ether, Mind, Understanding, and Thought of an I.

5. This is the lower. But know that I have another and higher nature than this, one of Elemental Soul, O mighty-armed one, and thereby is upheld this universe.

6. Learn that from these twain are sprung all born beings; the source of the whole universe and its dissolution am I."

ZOROASTRIANISM

The sacred books of Zoroastrianism are known as the *Avesta* or the *Zend-Avesta,* more accurately "the *Avesta,* or sacred text, and its *zend,* or interpretation." "The Avesta consists of four chief divisions, or groups of texts, all more or less fragmentary and varying in antiquity. These are: the *Yasna,* which is the chief liturgical work and includes the *Gathas* or hymns ascribed to Zoroaster as author, forming thus the oldest portion of the Avesta; the *Vispered* or supplementary ritual; the *Yashts,* which are hymns to angels or lesser divinities; the *Vendidad,* which contains the account of creation, and historical and homiletic matter. There are also minor divisions." *Yasna* means "worship including sacrifice."

The Yasna

1,21: If I have offended Thee, whether by thought, or word, or deed, whether by act of will, or without intent or wish, I earnestly make up the deficiency of this in praise to Thee. If I have caused decrease in that which is Thy Yasna, and Thy homage, I announce (and celebrate) to Thee (the more for this)!

12,1: I drive the Daevas hence; I confess as a Mazda-worshipper of the order of Zarathustra, estranged from the Daevas, devoted to the lore of the Lord, a praiser of the Bountiful Immortals; and to Ahura Mazda, the good and endowed with good possessions, I attribute all things good, to the holy One, the resplendent, to the glorious, whose are all things whatsoever which are good; whose is the Kine, whose is Asha (the righteous order pervading all things pure), whose are the stars, in whose light the glorious beings and objects are clothed.

57,4: We worship Sraosha, Obedience the blessed, and that lofty Lord who is Ahura Mazda Himself, Him who has attained the most to this our ritual, Him who has approached the nearest to us in our celebrations. And we worship all the words of Zarathustra, and all the deeds well done (for him), both those that have been done (in times gone by) and those which are yet to be done (for him in times to come).

The Vendidad

3,40–42: When is it so?

"It is so, if the sinner be a professor of the Religion of Mazda, or one who has been taught in it.

"But if he be not a professor of the Religion of Mazda, nor one who has been taught in it, then his sin is taken from him, if he makes confession of the Religion of Mazda and resolves never to commit again such forbidden deeds.

"The Religion of Mazda indeed, O Spitama Zarathustra! takes away from him who makes confession of it the bonds of his sin; it takes away breach of trust; it takes away murdering one of the faithful; it takes away burying a corpse; it takes away deeds for which there is no atonement; it takes away the worst sin of usury; it takes away any sin that may be sinned."

SHINTO

The two basic writings of Shinto are the *Ko-ji-ki* or "Records of Ancient Matters" and the *Nihon-gi* or the "Chronicles of Japan."

Ko-ji-ki

Volume I—Preface

I Yasumaro say:

Now when chaos had begun to condense, but force and form were not yet manifest, and there was nought named, nought done, who could know its shape? Nevertheless Heaven and Earth first parted, and the Three Deities performed the commencement of creation; the Passive and Active Essences then developed, and the Two Spirits became the ancestors of all things. Therefore did he enter obscurity and emerge into light, and the Sun and Moon were revealed by the washing of his eyes; he floated on and plunged into the sea-water, and Heavenly and Earthly Deities appeared through the ablution of his person. So in the dimness of the great commencement, we, by relying on the original teaching, learn the time of the conception of the earth and of the birth of islands; in the remoteness of the original beginning, we, by trusting the former sages, perceive the era of the genesis of Deities and the establishment of men. . . .

. . . So from the Deity Master-of-the-August-Centre-of-Heaven down to His Augustness Prince-

Wave - Limit - Brave - Cormorant - Thatch - Meeting-Incompletely makes the First Volume; from the Heavenly Sovereign Kamu-Yamato-Ihare-Biko down to the august reign of Homuda makes the Second Volume; from the Emperor Oho-Sazaki down to the great palace of Woharida makes the Third Volume. Altogether I have written Three Volumes, which I reverently and respectfully present. I Yasumaro, with true trembling and true fear, bow my head, bow my head.

Volume I, Section 3

Hereupon all the Heavenly Deities commanded the two Deities His Augustness the Male-Who-Invites and Her Augustness the Female-Who-Invites, ordering them to "make, consolidate, and give birth to this drifting land." Granting them an heavenly jewelled spear, they (thus) deigned to charge them. So the two Deities, standing upon the Floating Bridge of Heaven, pushed down the jewelled spear and stirred with it, whereupon, when they had stirred the brine till it went curdlecurdle, and drew (the spear) up, the brine that dripped down from the end of the spear was piled up and became an island. That is the island of Onogoro.

Nihon-gi

55. "The Yemishi rebelled. Tamichi was sent to attack them. He was worsted by the Yemishi, and slain at the harbour of Ishimi. Now one of his fol-

lowers obtained Tamichi's armlet and gave it to his wife, who embraced the armlet and strangled herself. When the men of that time heard of this they shed tears."

TAOISM

The great classic of Taoism is the *Tao-Teh-King*, the "Canon of Reason and Virtue." This writing is generally conceded to have been done directly by Lao-tze sometime during the first half of the sixth century B.C. It consists of wise sayings and generalizations.

The Tao Teh King

2. The Beautiful being once recognized as such by the world, the Repulsive appears. Goodness being once recognized as such, Evil appears in the like manner. Thus existence and non-existence produce each other; the difficult and the easy bring about each other; the long and the short impart form to each other; the high and the low comply with each other; sounds and voices harmonize with each other; priority and sequence alternate with each other.

Wherefore the Sage pursues a policy of inaction, and teaches men in silence;

He forms all things without shrinking; produces them without claiming the possession (of virtue); acts without presuming on (his ability); and completes his achievements without taking any credit to himself. It is only he who thus does not stand upon his merit; and therefore his merit does not depart from him.

4. The Tao is full; yet in operation as though not self-elated. In its origin it is as it were the Ancestor of All Things. It chastens asperity; it unravels confusion; it moderates the radiance (proceeding from those in whom Tao is embodied); and it identifies itself with the sordid ones (of the earth). Pellucid (as a spreading ocean) it yet has the semblance of permanence. I know not whose offspring it is. Its "idea" existed before God was.

34. The Great Tao is all-pervasive; it may be seen on the right and on the left.

All things depend on it, and are produced; it denies itself to none.

It achieves its works of merit, but has no name or reputation. With tenderness it nourishes all things, yet claims no lordship over them.

It is ever passionless, and may be named among the smallest things.

All things submit to it, yet it claims no lordship over them; it may be called great.

Thus the Sage to the end of his life never exalts himself; and thus he is able to achieve great things.

62. Tao is the deep reservoir of all things. It is the jewel of the good man, and guardian of the bad.

Virtuous words are marketable; honourable deeds may be made over to the credit of others. What reason is there for casting a man off on account of his being unvirtuous? . . .

It was this Tao that the ancients reverenced. Why do not (the rulers of today) strive daily to acquire it?

JAINISM

There are three sacred scriptures of Jainism which are of particular importance. The first is the *Ayaranya Sutra* (also called the *Samayika*), which deals with the problem of conduct. The second is the *Sutrakritanga*, which contains refutations of heretical doctrines, discussions on holy living, matters of punishment and the praise of Mahavira. The *Uttaradhyayana Sutra* contains instruction, encouragement and warning for the young monk.

The Ayaranya Sutra

1,2,2,1: A wise man should remove any aversion (to control); he will be liberated in the proper time. . . . Those who are freed (from attachment to the world and its pleasures), reach the opposite shore. Subduing desire by desirelessness, he does not enjoy the pleasures that offer themselves. Desireless, giving up the world, and ceasing to act, he knows, and sees, and has no wishes because of his discernment; he is called houseless.

1,6,4,2: Those who deserve to be called fools, are born again and again. Standing low (in learning or control) they will exalt themselves (and say) in their pride: I am learned. They speak harshly unto the passionless; they upbraid them with their former trades, or revile them with untrue reproaches. The wise, therefore, should know the law.

Sacred Literature

The Sutrakritanga

1,1,2,26–29: There are three ways of committing sins: by one's own activity, by commission, by approval (of the deed).

These are the three ways of committing sins. Thus by purity of the heart one reaches Nirvana.

A layman may kill his son (during a famine) and eat him; a wise (monk) who partakes of the meat, will not be defiled by the sin.

The mind of those who sin in thoughts is not pure; they are wrong, they do not conduct themselves carefully.

1,9,3,5: The iniquity of all these men who cling to property goes on increasing; for those who procure themselves pleasures by sinful acts will not get rid of misery.

The Uttaradhyayana Sutra

18,33: A wise man believes in the existence of the soul, he avoids the heresy of the non-existence of the soul; possessing true faith one should practice the very difficult Law according to the faith.

19,25: Impartiality towards all beings in the world, whether friends or enemies, and abstention from injury to living beings through the whole life: this is a difficult duty.

BUDDHISM

The sacred scriptures of Buddhism are the *Tripitaka* or "Three Baskets" of teachings and the

Dhammapada, a collection of the sayings of Buddha. The *Tripitaka* are the *Vinaya Pitaka* or Discipline Basket, the *Sutta Pitaka* or Teaching Basket, and the *Abhidhamma Pitaka* or Metaphysical Basket.

The Vinaya Pitaka

5,1,25: When a Bhikkhu, Lord, has thus become fully emancipated in heart, even though many objects visible to the sight should enter the path of his eye, yet they take not possession of his mind: undefiled is his mind, firm, immovable; and he sees into the (manner in which that impression) passes away— even though many objects audible to the ear, smell-able to the nostrils, tasteable to the tongue, feelable to the body, sensible to the intellect should enter upon the path of the ear, the nose, the tongue, the skin, the intellect, yet they take not possession of his mind: undefiled is his mind, firm, immovable, and he sees into the (manner in which that impression) passes away.

The Sutta Pitaka

1,14: There the Blessed One stayed in the king's house and held that comprehensive religious talk with the brethren on the nature of upright conduct, and of earnest contemplation, and of intelligence. "Great is the fruit, great the advantage of earnest contemplation when set round with upright conduct. Great is the fruit, great the advantage of intellect when set round with earnest contemplation. The mind set round with intelligence is freed from the great evils, that is to say, from sensuality, from individuality, from delusion, and from ignorance."

The Dhammapada

1. Mind it is which gives to things their quality, their foundation, and their being: whoso speaks or acts with impure mind, him sorrow dogs, as the wheel follows the steps of the draught-ox.

5. Never does hatred cease by hating; by not hating does it cease: this is the ancient law.

11. Those who mistake the shadow for the substance, and the substance for the shadow, never attain the reality, following wandering fires (being followers of a false pursuit).

12. But if a man knows the substance and the shadow as they are, he attains the reality, following the true trail.

19. If a man is a great preacher of the sacred text, but slothful and no doer of it, he is a hireling shepherd, who has no part in the flock.

20. If a man preaches but a little of the text and practices the teaching, putting away lust and hatred and infatuation; if he is truly wise and detached and seeks nothing here or hereafter, his lot is with the holy ones.

21. Zeal is the way to Nirvana. Sloth is the way of death. The zealous die not: the slothful are as it were dead.

382. Let the young Bhikku apply himself to Bud-

dha's Preaching: so will he light up the world as the moon escaped from the clouds.

CONFUCIANISM

The so-called "Classics" of Confucianism number six and were compiled by Confucius out of the sacred lore of the ancient Chinese religion. They are the *Shu King* (Book of History), the *Shih King* (Book of Poetry), the *I King* (Book of Changes), the *Li Ki* (Book of Rites), the *Ch'un Ch'iu* (Spring and Autumn Annals), and the *Hsiao King* (Book of Filial Piety). A second group is known as "The Four Books." These are the *Ta Hsio* (Great Learning), the *Chung Yung* (Doctrines of the Mean), the *Lun Yu* (the Analects), and the *Meng-tze* (Book of Mencius).

The Shu King

4,8,2,1: For all affairs let there be adequate preparation—with preparation there will be no calamitous issue. Do not open the door for favorites, from whom you will receive contempt. Do not be ashamed of mistakes, and (go on to) make them crimes. Let your mind rest in its proper objects, and the affairs of your government will be pure. Officiousness in sacrificing is called irreverence; and multiplying ceremonies leads to disorder. To serve the spirits acceptably (in this way) is difficult.

5,10,2: . . . above all, do you strictly keep yourself from drink.

The Shih King

ODE 7. THE WO KIANG

I have brought my offerings,
A ram and a bull.
May Heaven accept them!

I imitate and follow and observe the statutes of king
Wan,
Seeking daily to secure the tranquility of the kingdom.
King Wan, the Blesser, has descended on the right,
and accepted.
Do I not, night and day,
Revere the majesty of Heaven,
Thus to preserve (its favour)?

The Lun Yu

1,8,1–4: The Master said, "If the scholar be not grave, he will not call forth any veneration, and his learning will not be solid.

"Hold faithfulness and sincerity as first principles.

"Have no friends not equal to yourself.

"When you have faults, do not fear to abandon them."

14,29: The Master said, "The superior man is modest in his speech, but exceeds in his actions."

15,14: The Master said, "He who requires much from himself and little from others, will keep himself from being the object of resentment."

ISLAM

Mohammed gave the name *Koran* (Arabic *Qur'an*, from *qara'a*, to read) to "a single revelation or a collection of revelations, but after his death, when his various utterances had been collected in writing, this name was applied to the whole book." However, there remained a doubt as to just what the prophet did say. On this Dr. S. E. Frost comments in his book *The Sacred Writings of the World's Great Religions*: "Consequently, some twelve years later, Othman, third caliph, commanded that all copies of the original work be destroyed and a new authentic version be prepared. This accepted volume contains scraps of beliefs from many religious sources, chief of which are Arabic traditions and folk lore, Zoroastrianism, the Jewish and Christian theology." The Koran has 114 chapters or *suras* of which the first is the *fatihah* (that which opens), the prayer used by all Moslems.

The Koran

Sura I

1. Praise be to God, Lord of the worlds!
2. The compassionate, the merciful!
3. King on the day of reckoning!
4. Thee only do we worship, and to Thee do we cry for help.
5. Guide Thou us on the straight path,
6. The path of those to whom Thou hast been

gracious—with whom Thou art not angry, and who go not astray.

SURA II

1. No doubt is there about this Book: It is a guidance to the God-fearing,

2. Who believe in the unseen, who observe prayer, and out of what we have bestowed on them, expend for God; . . .

99. The unbelievers among the people of the Book, and among the idolaters, desire not that any good should be sent down to you from your Lord: but God will shew His special mercy to whom He will, for He is of great bounty.

100. Whatsoever verses we cancel, or cause thee to forget, we bring a better or its like. Knowest thou not that God hath power over all things? . . .

103. Many of the people of the Book desire to bring you back to unbelief after ye have believed, out of selfish envy, even after the truth hath been clearly shewn them. But forgive them, and shun them till God shall come in with His working. . . .

105. And they say, "None but Jews or Christians shall enter Paradise": This is their wish. Say: Give your proofs if ye speak the truth. . . .

113. Verily, with the Truth have we sent thee, a bearer of good tidings and a warner: and of the people of Hell thou shalt not be questioned.

114. But until thou follow their religion, neither Jews nor Christians will be satisfied with thee. Say: Verily, guidance of God—that is the guidance! And

if, after "the Knowledge" which hath reached thee, thou follow their desires, thou shalt find neither helper nor protector against God. . . .

158. Your God is one God: there is no God but He, the Compassionate, the Merciful.

Sura V

17. And of those who say, "We are Christians," have we accepted the covenant. But they too have forgotten a part of what they were taught; wherefore we have stirred up enmity and hatred among them that shall last till the day of the Resurrection; and in the end will God tell them of their doings.

18. O people of the Scriptures! now is our Apostle come to you to clear up to you much that ye concealed of those Scriptures, and to pass over many things. Now hath a light and a clear Book come to you from God, by which God will guide him who shall follow after His good pleasure, to paths of peace, and will bring them out of the darkness to the light, by His will: and to the straight path will He guide them.

19. Infidels now are they who say, "Verily God is the Messiah Ibn Maryam (son of Mary)!" Say: And who could aught obtain from God, if He chose to destroy the Messiah Ibn Maryam, and his mother, and all who are on the earth together? . . .

21. Say the Jews and the Christians, "Sons are we of God and His beloved." Say: Why then doth He chastise you for your sins? Nay! ye are but a part of the men whom He hath created! He will

pardon whom He pleaseth, and with God is the sovereignty of the Heavens and the Earth, and of all that is between them, and unto Him shall all things return.

22. O people of the Book! now hath our Apostle come to you to clear up to you the cessation of Apostles, lest you should say, "There hath come to us no bearer of good tidings, nor any warner." But now hath a bearer of good tidings and a warner reached you. And God is Almighty.

Sura XXII

40. A sanction is given to those who, because they have suffered outrages, have taken up arms; and verily, God is well able to succor them.

Sura XXIII

1. Happy now the BELIEVERS,
2. Who humble them in their prayer,
3. And who keep aloof from vain words,
4. And who are doers of alms deeds,
5. And who restrain their appetites,
6. (Save with their wives, or the slaves whom their right hands possess: for in that case they shall be free from blame:
7. But they whose desires reach further than this are transgressors:)
8. And who tend well their trusts and their covenants,
9. And who keep them strictly to their prayers:

10. These shall be the heritors, Who shall inherit the paradise, to abide therein for ever.

Sura XLIX

15. True believers are those only who believe in God and His Apostle, and afterwards doubt not; and who contend with their substance and their persons on the path of God. These are the sincere.

SIKHISM

The following is part of a document which all Sikhs repeat each morning and which is considered by them to be the key to their Scriptures. It is believed to have been written by Nanak.

The Japji

Preamble: There is but one God whose name is true, the Creator, devoid of fear and enmity, immortal, unborn, self-existent; by the favour of the Guru.

Repeat His Name

The True One was in the beginning; the True One was in the primal age.

The True One is now also, O Nanak; the True One who also shall be.

1. By thinking I cannot obtain a conception of Him, even though I think hundreds of thousands of times.

Even though I be silent and keep my attention firmly fixed on Him, I cannot preserve silence.

The hunger of the hungry for God subsideth not, though they obtain the load of the worlds.

If man should have thousands and hundreds of thousands of devices, even one would not assist him in obtaining God.

How shall man become true before God? How shall the veil of falsehood be rent?

By walking, O Nanak, according to the will of the Commander as pre-ordained.

3. Who can sing His power? Who hath power to sing it?

Who can sing His gifts or know His signs?

Who can sing His attributes, His greatness, and His deeds?

Who can sing His knowledge whose study is arduous?

Who can sing Him, who fashioneth the body and again destroyeth it?

Who can sing Him, who taketh away life and again restoreth it?

Who can sing Him, who appeareth to be far, but is known to be near?

Who can sing Him, who is all-seeing and omnipresent?

In describing Him there would never be an end.

Millions of men give millions upon millions of descriptions of Him, but they fail to describe Him.

The Giver giveth; the receiver groweth weary of receiving.

In every age man subsisteth by His bounty.

The Commander by His order hath laid out the way of the world.

Nanak, God the unconcerned is happy.

He is not established, nor is He created.

The pure one existeth by Himself.

They who worshipped Him have obtained honour.

Nanak, sing His praises who is the Treasury of excellences.

Sing and hear and put His love into your hearts.

Thus shall your sorrows be removed, and you shall be absorbed in Him who is the abode of happiness.

Under the Guru's instruction God's word is heard; under the Guru's instruction its knowledge is acquired; under the Guru's instruction man learns that God is everywhere contained.

CHAPTER THREE

Topical Comparison

DEITIES WORSHIPPED

Man, after the fall, changed the glory of the incorruptible God for the likeness of an image of corruptible man, of birds, four-footed beasts, and creeping things (Rom. 1:22, 23). These are classified today under the heading of nature-worship. Naturism includes also the worship of the sun, moon, and stars, of trees and even stones as well as animals. Since all of these are looked upon as spirit-animated, they are usually placed under the more general category of Animism. Different schools of thought vary in their divisions and sub-divisions, but suffice it to say here that included in this are Ancestor Worship, Totemism, Fetishism (where material objects are considered spirit-indwelt, and become charms, amulets or talismans), and certain forms of magic and taboo. Many of these features can be traced in the living religions of today even though a supreme deity is worshipped, only we call them superstitions.

JUDAISM—The worship of one God, "The Supreme Being, regarded as the Creator, Author, and First Cause of the universe, the Ruler of the world and the affairs of men, the Supreme Judge and Father, tempering justice with mercy, working out His purposes through chosen agents—individuals as well as nations—and communicating His will through prophets and other appointed channels."—*Jewish Encyclopedia.*

CHRISTIANITY—The worship of the one and the same God revealed to Israel in her Sacred Scriptures but understood to be so revealed as a tri-unity of Persons known primarily as Father, Son, and Holy Spirit.

HINDUISM—The earliest worship was animistic but came to be centered in one supreme impersonal cosmic Being known as Brahma. Popular Hinduism is essentially polytheistic, but reformed theistic Hinduism conceives of God as comprising a triad of Brahma (Creator), Vishnu (Preserver), and Siva (Destroyer).

ZOROASTRIANISM—The worship of one cosmic Power or Lord of light and goodness called Ahura Mazda (Ormazd), who is, however, not absolutely supreme because of the co-existing cosmic Power of darkness and evil called Angra Mainyu (Ahriman).

SHINTO—The original worship of Shinto was Naturism, the chief deity being Ama-terasu (the Heaven-Shining-One, the Sun-goddess) of whom the first Mikado was supposed to have been a literal descendant. Thus emperor worship developed. But myriads of deities are worshipped, chief among them being Izanagi (the Male-who-invites) and Izanami (the Female-who-invites).

TAOISM—The worship of the Tao (Way), the moral and physical order of the world, especially the path of truth and virtue. The Tao-Teh-King sets forth the Tao as an eternal, impersonal, mystical Supreme Being. But Taoism today has degenerated into a polytheistic occultism of the lowest order.

JAINISM—Mahavira taught that there was no object of worship; that no deity should be prayed to or even talked about. However, his followers deified him and worship his image.

BUDDHISM—Buddha, like Mahavira, taught no dependence upon one Supreme Being but came himself to be deified and worshipped. Numerous other deities are worshipped today by the majority of Buddhists.

CONFUCIANISM—Confucius taught that there was one Supreme Being, to be designated either personally as Supreme Ruler or impersonally as Heaven. In China this one person came to be the Emperor. Popular Confucianism embraces both Naturism and Ancestor-worship.

ISLAM—The worship of Allah as the one and only Supreme Being.

SIKHISM—The worship of the one God who is called True.

BELIEF CONCERNING SIN

JUDAISM—"SIN: Under the Jewish theocracy, wilful disregard of the positive, or wilful infraction of the negative, commands of God as proclaimed by Moses and interpreted by the Rabbis."—*Jewish Encyclopedia.*

CHRISTIANITY—"Sin is lack of conformity to the moral law of God, either in act, disposition, or state" (A. H. Strong's *Systematic Theology*). It is defined as lawlessness (I John 3:4, ASV), unrighteousness (I John 5:17), lack of faith (Rom. 14:23), and knowing good but not doing it (James 4:17). Acts of sin are the expression of a sin nature resident in all men.

HINDUISM—Disobedience to law, especially the law of caste. This, however, is a defect rather than a sin, as is philosophic ignorance, and results in reincarnations.

ZOROASTRIANISM—Evil thoughts and acts arise from the influence of evil spirits (*Daeva,* later *Diu*). Among these demons are Wrath, Greed, Arrogance, False Speech, Harlot, etc.

SHINTO—Shinto has no definite moral code except obedience to the Emperor. Personal physical cleanliness is stressed rather than heart purity.

TAOISM—There is little here about sin or any particular morality, the chief ethical idea being that of inactivity, quietness, calm, and simplicity.

JAINISM—Mahavira stressed five vows which prohibited killing, lying, stealing, sexual pleasures, and all attachments (including love and hate).

BUDDHISM—Evil consists in the desire for any kind of individual existence or activity, but there is no sin against a Divine Being. It is the thought of self which mars everything. There are five prohibitions for all Buddhists—do not kill, steal, commit adultery, lie, or drink intoxicants. Five more are required of monastics—abstinence (1) from eating at forbidden times; (2) from dancing, singing, music, and seeing spectacles; (3) from garlands, scents, unguents, ornaments, and finery; (4) from high or broad beds; (5) from accepting gold or silver.

CONFUCIANISM—Here the tendency of man's nature is seen as good, and there is no consideration of or provision for moral evil. Its ethics consist in social propriety, what is known as the principle of reciprocal propriety: "What you do not want done to yourselves, do not do to others."

ISLAM—The five essential duties of Islam are the repetition of the creed, prayer, almsgiving, prescribed fasting and a pilgrimage to Mecca. Abstinence from these is sin. Numerous other things are listed as resulting in punishment, such as slander, backbiting, lying, insolence, etc., but especially all unbelief in Allah and the Koran.

SIKHISM—Sin consists primarily in forgetting the True Name: "They who forget the Name, go astray. . . ."

METHOD OF SALVATION

JUDAISM—Early in the history of Judaism the laws for the various offerings were given. Sin was atoned for by the blood of the sin-offering (Lev. 4 and 5). "With the fall of the Temple and the cessation of the atonement offerings, the importance of repentance as a means of expiation became inevitably enhanced" (A. Cohen, *Everyman's Talmud*). Johanan b. Zakkai declared works of benevolence to have atoning powers as great as those of sacrifice. Also, in place of the sacrifices, "the Synagogue Ritual of the Day of Atonement became in the popular mind the supreme path to purification from sin" (A. Cohen). Also considered to have atoning efficacy are fasting, suffering, and the study of the law.

CHRISTIANITY—After mentioning works of benevolence as having atoning power, the *Jewish Encyclopedia* goes on to say: "This view, however, did not solve satisfactorily for all the problem of sin—the evil rooted in man from the very beginning, from the fall of Adam (IV Esd. iii. 20, vii. 118). Hence a large number of Jews accepted the Christian faith in the Atonement by the blood 'shed for many for the remission of sins' (Matt. xxvi. 28; Heb. x. 12; Col. i. 20) or in Jesus as 'the Lamb of God' (John i. 29; Apoc. of John vii. 14, and elsewhere)." This accurately expresses the evangelical Christian view of justification through faith in Christ. The Roman Catholic position, however, is that both faith and a life of good works are necessary if one is to be justified in God's sight.

HINDUISM—The Rig-Veda sets forth prayer as the chief method of salvation. According to Brahmanas the Asva-medha (horse-sacrifice) is the atonement for everything and redeems all sin. Salvation from repeated reincarnations becomes possible by a quiet unstriving consciousness of freedom from all changes, and absorption in Brahma.

ZOROASTRIANISM—Various formulas are prescribed as efficacious for cleansing from all sin. Praise is especially advocated as meritorious. If one is not a professor of the religion of Mazda, then his sin will be removed if he makes such a confession and resolves never to commit such sin again.

SHINTO—The ceremony of Oho-harahi (The Great Purification) includes a preliminary lustration, expiatory offerings, and the recitation of a formula in which the Mikado, on the authority transmitted to him from the Sun-goddess, declares to his people the absolution of all their sins.

TAOISM—There is no sin-consciousness in Taoism, and what would be considered salvation is the attainment of the abiding quietude of the eternal Tao. This is accomplished by compliance with the Tao and possessing Tao. "When the faculty of knowledge and the placidity blend together, they nourish each other; then from the nature there comes forth harmony and orderly method. The attributes (of the Tao) constitute harmony; the Tao (itself) secures the orderly method. When the attributes appear in a universal practice of forbearance, we have Benevolence; when the path is all marked by orderly method, we have Righteousness; when the righteousness is clearly manifested, and all things are regarded with affection, we have Loyal-heartedness; when the (heart's) core is thus (pure) and real, and carried back to its (proper) qualities, we have Music; and when this sincerity appears in all the range of the capacity, and its demonstrations are in accordance with what is elegant, we have Ceremony" (Writings of Kwang-Tze).

JAINISM—Salvation is found in asceticism. By conquering love, hate, and wrong belief a person will cut off the fetters of Karma (the moral law of retribution for deeds done which causes rebirth into this same miserable world).

BUDDHISM—Release from Karma becomes possible by the suppression of all desires and when one has ceased to think of good and evil and has risen above them both. The result is Nirvana, a negative state of passionless peace.

CONFUCIANISM—"Zeal is the way to Nirvana.... The wise who know the power of zeal delight in it.... These wise ones by meditation and reflection, by constant effort reach Nirvana, highest freedom" (From the Dhammapada).

ISLAM—Salvation according to this faith is expressed in the word Mohammed used to designate his religion—*islam* ("submission" to God).

SIKHISM—Salvation consists in knowing God and being absorbed in Him. It is not obtained by mere works but by God's grace. The Kind One saves those on whom He looks with favour.

BELIEF CONCERNING THE FUTURE LIFE

JUDAISM—The position of modern Judaism is expressed by Morris Joseph in *Judaism as Creed and Life* as follows: "Judaism, when at its best, has steadily kept before it this idea of the spirituality of the future recompense. Such notions as that of a Resurrection of the body, of physical torments for the sinner, of a celestial playground, the scene of more or less sensuous pleasures, have found a place in certain phases of Jewish doctrine; but they have been rejected one by one by the best Jewish teachers." *The Jewish Encyclopedia* describes the views through the Talmudic period to have been the following. "Gehinnon has seven names: 'Sheol,' 'Abbadon,' 'Pit of Corruption,' 'Mire of Clay,' 'Shadow of Death,' and 'Nether Parts of the Earth.' . . . It is also called 'Tophet.' . . . It has seven departments, one beneath the other (Sotah 10b). There are seven kinds of pain (IV Esd. vii. 81 *et seq.*). . . . The Garden of Eden is called the 'Garden of Righteousness'. . . being no longer an earthly paradise. . . . It is above the earth, and its inhabitants are 'clothed with garments of light and eternal life, and eat of the tree of life' . . . in the company of the Lord and His anointed. . . . As the wicked have a sevenfold pain, the righteous have a sevenfold joy. . . . There are seven divisions for the righteous. . . . Each of the righteous will have a mansion, and God will talk with them and lead them in a dance. . ." (Article on "Eschatology"). "Nevertheless the prevailing rabbinical conception of the future is that of the world of resurrection, not that of pure immortality . . . just as the Church knows only of a future based on the resurrection . . . while the dogma of resurrection was gradually discarded and, in the Reform rituals, eliminated from the prayer books" (Article on "Immortality").

CHRISTIANITY—The New Testament teaches the resurrection of both the just and the unjust, with eternal bliss in heaven for the redeemed and eternal punishment for the lost in hell. *The Augsburg Confession,* presented to Emperor Charles V at the Diet of Augsburg in 1530, states in Article XVII: "Christ shall appear to judge and shall raise up all the dead, and shall give unto the godly and elect eternal life and everlasting joys; but ungodly men and the devils shall he condemn unto endless torments." *The Westminster Confession of Faith* (1647), Chapter XXXIII: "For then shall the righteous go into everlasting life, and receive fulness of joy and refreshing which shall come from the presence of the Lord; but the wicked, who know not God, and obey not the gospel of Jesus Christ, shall be cast into eternal torments, and be punished with everlasting destruction from the presence of the Lord, and from the glory of his power." *The New Hampshire Baptist Confession* (1833): ". . . the wicked will be adjudged to endless punishment, and the righteous to endless joy; and that this judgment will fix forever the final state of men in heaven or hell, on principles of righteousness."

HINDUISM—Webster defines *karma* in Hinduism and Buddhism as "the principle of causality, the whole ethical consequence of one's acts considered as fixing one's lot in the future existence; the continuous working of every thought, word, or deed throughout eternity in a kind of moral causal sequence." In Hinduism this "law of deeds" results in repeated reincarnations to lower or higher social status, but can be overcome by abstaining from all efforts and desires and thus entering the state of impersonality.

Other concepts, however, are found as the statement of Nachiketas in the Katha Upanishad, "In the heaven-world there is no fear; thou art not there, O Death, and no one is afraid on account of old age. Leaving behind both hunger and thirst, and out of reach of sorrow, all rejoice in the world of heaven."

ZOROASTRIANISM—"(Yea) when the two spirits came together at the first to make life, and life's absence, and to determine how the world at the last shall be (ordered), for the wicked (Hell) the worst life, for the holy (Heaven) the Best Mental State" (Yasna 30,4).

SHINTO—What little teaching on the future life that is found here is Hinduistic and Buddhistic.

TAOISM—Very indefinite concepts exist here. Immortal life is merely a protracted existence.

JAINISM—The same view as in Hinduism.

BUDDHISM—The same view as in Hinduism, the term *Nirvana* being used for the state of passionless peace.

CONFUCIANISM—Here there is no teaching of a better form of life after death nor any concept of punishment. There is some thought that the dead continue in existence and hover around the family abode or the grave and therefore on stated occasions food is placed before them as sort of a communion meal.

ISLAM—In chapter 36 of the Koran we read: "On this day (of the resurrection) no soul shall be unjustly treated in the least; neither shall ye be rewarded, but according to what ye have wrought. On this day the inhabitants of Paradise shall be wholly taken up with joy; they and their wives shall rest in shady groves, leaning on magnificant couches. There shall they have fruit, and they shall obtain whatever they shall desire. Peace shall be the word spoken unto the righteous, by a merciful Lord: but he shall say unto the wicked, Be ye separated this day, O ye wicked, from the righteous. . . . This is hell, with which ye were threatened: be cast into the same this day, to be burned; for that ye have been unbelievers."

SIKHISM—Here again we have the same pantheistic merging of the self into the infinite as in Hinduism and Buddhism. Yet we read in Slok VI of the Asa Ki War, "Many depart from here after eating what they had amassed in previous births; shall they have any business whatever in the next world? . . . Saith Nanak, the saints hunger to praise Thee; the true Name is their support. In everlasting joy they abide day and night. . . ."

THE GOLDEN RULE

It will be noted that some of these statements are actually the Silver Rule, which is similar to the Golden Rule but viewed from the negative viewpoint.

JUDAISM—"What thou thyself hatest, do to no man" (Tobit 4:15). There is a distinction shown in the Babylonian Talmud between the gentleness of Hillel and the impatience of Shammai, and one of the examples is the following: "On another occasion it happened that a certain heathen came before Shammai and said to him, 'Make me a proselyte, on condition that you teach me the whole Torah while I stand on one foot.' Thereupon he repulsed him with the builder's cubit which was in his hand. When he went before Hillel, he [Hillel] said to him, 'What is hateful to you, do not to your neighbour: that is the whole Torah, while the rest is the commentary thereof; go and learn it' " (Shabbath 31a).

CHRISTIANITY—"Therefore all things whatsoever ye would that men should do to you, do ye even so to them: for this is the law and the prophets" (Matt. 7:12).

HINDUISM—"Do naught to others which, if done to thee, would cause thee pain: this is the sum of duty" (Mahabbarata 5:1517).

ZOROASTRIANISM—"Whatever thou dost not approve for thyself, do not approve for anyone else. When thou hast acted in this manner, thou art righteous" (24:330 in *Sacred Books of the East,* by F. Max Miller, 50 volumes, Oxford). "That nature only is good when it shall not do unto another whatever is not good for its own self" (*SBE,* 18:271).

TAOISM—"Recompense injury with kindness" (*SBE,* 39:105).

JAINISM—"Impartiality towards all beings in the world, whether friends or enemies, and abstention from injury to living beings throughout the whole life: this is a difficult duty" (Uttaradhyayana Sutra, 19:25).

BUDDHISM—"In five ways should a clansman minister to his friends and familiars, . . . by treating them as he treats himself" (Sigalovada Sutta, 31). "Is there a deed, Rahula, thou dost wish to do? Then bethink thee thus: 'Is this deed conducive to my own harm, or to others harm, or to that of both?' Then this is a bad deed, entailing suffering. Such a deed must thou surely not do" (Majjhima Nikaya, 1:415, *Buddhism* by R. Davids).

CONFUCIANISM—"What you do not want done to yourself, do not do to others" (Analects, 15:23). "Tsze-kung said, 'What I do not wish men to do to me, I also wish not to do to men.' The Master said, 'Ts'ze, you have not attained to that' " (Analects, 5:11).

ISLAM—There is here no statement of the Golden Rule as applying to others generally, but to a brother in particular: "Help thy brother, be he transgressed, or transgressor, and he will help you in like."

It is interesting to note that variations of this rule appear elsewhere also. Isocrates said, "Do not do to others what you would not wish to suffer yourself" (*Nicocles, or the Cyprians*). Aristotle: "Treat your friends as you want them to treat you" (As given in *Lives and Opinions of Eminent Philosophers*). Philo: "Do not do what any one is vexed to suffer" (As reported in *Eusebius*).

LIBERALITY

JUDAISM—"R. Assi said: A man should never neglect to give the third of a shekel (for charity) in a year. . . . R. Assi further said: Charity is equivalent to all the other religious precepts combined. . . R. Eleazar said: He who causes others to do good is greater than the doer. . . . R. Eleazar further said: When the Temple stood, a man used to bring his shekel and so make atonement. Now that the Temple no longer stands, if they give for charity, well and good, and if not, the heathens will come and take from them forcibly. And even so it will be reckoned to them as if they had given charity, as it is written, *(I will make) thine exactors righteousness*" (Baba Bathra, 9a).

CHRISTIANITY—"Give and it shall be given unto you. . . . For with the same measure that ye mete withal it shall be measured to you again" (Luke 6:38). ". . . he that giveth, let him do it with simplicity" (Rom. 12:8). "Every man according as he purposeth in his heart, so let him give; not grudgingly, or of necessity: for God loveth a cheerful giver" (II Cor. 9:7). "As we have therefore opportunity, let us do good unto all men, especially unto them who are of the household of faith" (Gal. 6:10).

HINDUISM—"Bounteous is he who gives unto the beggar who comes to him in want of food and feeble. Success attends him in the shout of battle. He makes a friend of him in future troubles. . . . Let the rich satisfy the poor implorer . . . the liberal friend outvalues him who gives not" (Rig-Veda X. 117. 3, 5, 7). "The gift that is given as a duty to one who cannot make return, with fitness of place, time, and person, is known as a gift of the goodness-mood. But that which is for the sake of reward or in view of fruit thereafter, or is grudged in the giving, is known as a gift of the mood of fieriness" (Bhagavad-Gita, XVII. 20, 21).

ZOROASTRIANISM—"The gifts of Vohn-mano to the deeds done in this world for Mazda! He who relieves the poor makes Ahura king" (Vendidad 19, 22).

SHINTO—"Be generous to all creatures, both human and animal. Long life is the reward of generous giving" (Oracle of Hachiman).

TAOISM—"Now there are three things which I regard as precious, which I grasp and prize. The first is compassion; the second is frugality; the third is not venturing to take precedence of others—modesty. I prize compassion; therefore I am able to be fearless. I prize frugality; therefore I am able to be liberal. I prize modesty; therefore I am able to become a leader of men" (Tao Teh King, 67).

BUDDHISM—"Misers go not to the realm of gods: therefore he is a fool who does not delight in liberality. The wise delighting in liberality come thereby with gladness to the other world" (Dhammapada, 177).

CONFUCIANISM—"The Master said, I have heard that a superior man helps the distressed, but does not add to the wealth of the rich" (Lun Yu, 6, 3, 2). "Mencius said: Benevolence overcomes its opposite even as water overcomes fire. But those who practice benevolence nowadays are taking a cup of water, as it were, to quench a cartload of burning fuel. Failing to extinguish the blaze, they say that water cannot overcome fire! This only helps the cause of those who are against benevolence altogether, and in the end their own benevolence will also disappear" (Meng-Tze, 6, 1, 18, 1–2).

ISLAM—"And as for him who voluntarily performeth a good work; verily God is grateful and knowing. . . . Contribute out of your substance towards the defence of the religion of God, and throw not yourselves with your own hands into perdition; and do good, for God loveth those who do good. . . . If there be any debtor under a difficulty of paying his debt, let his creditor wait till it be easy for him to do it; but if ye remit it as alms, it will be better for you, if ye knew it" (Koran, Sura II).

SIKHISM—"In the minds of the generous contentment is produced in their desire to give" (Asa Ki War, Slok VI). "Thou shalt obtain a reward in proportion to what thou hast done" (Asa Ki War, Pauri X).

CHAPTER FOUR

Distinctives of Christianity

THE DISTINCTIVE FEATURES OF CHRISTIANTY

Although the following features are listed as distinctive to Christianity, they all have their foundation in the Sacred Scriptures of Judaism. It is their development into various creedal statements which is peculiar to Christianity.

1. The concept of God as a tri-unity of three Persons generally spoken of as Father, Son and Holy Spirit.

2. The incarnation of one of these Divine Persons for the purpose of giving His life in substitutionary death as a ransom for sinners.

3. The actual physical resurrection of this Divine Redeemer.

4. The ascension of the Redeemer to heaven to officiate as High Priest in an intercessory capacity for those He has redeemed.

5. The distinctive ministry of the Holy Spirit.

6. The indwelling presence of the Father, the Son, and the Holy Spirit.

7. The eschatological system embracing a resurrection of the dead, a period of unequalled tribulation, and a millennial period with the re-established Davidic kingdom. (Some orthodox Christians spiritualize the Millennium rather than accepting it as a literal, future event.)

These seven features are characteristic of what is known as "orthodox" and "historic" Christianity.

Many forms of modern Christianity have departed, to different degrees, from these beliefs. Unitarianism denies all of them. But of historic Christianity Dr. Kaufmann Kohler, former Rabbi of Temple Beth-El, New York, and President of the Hebrew Union College, Cincinnati, Ohio, writes in a comparison of Christianity with Islam, "Leone del Bene (Judah Asahel Meha-Tob) also may be mentioned, who, in his *Kis 'ot le-Bet David,* 1646, xxiv., xxvi., xlvi., clviii., compares Mohammedanism with Christianity, and declares the latter as superior, notwithstanding its trinitarian dogma" (*Jewish Encyclopedia,* article on "Christianity").

THE DISTINCTIVE PERSON OF CHRISTIANITY

No founder of any religion has dared to claim for himself one fraction of the assertions made by the Lord Jesus Christ about himself. No religion has claimed for its founder what Christianity has claimed for the Lord Jesus Christ. No founder of any religion has been as highly acclaimed by those of other faiths as has the Lord Jesus Christ.

The Claims of Christ

John 10:33 tells in the words of others what Christ claimed for himself: "The Jews answered him, saying, For a good work we stone thee not; but for blasphemy; and because that thou, being a man, makest thyself God."

In a series of lectures at the University of Oxford, Canon H. P. Liddon spoke on "The Divinity of Our Lord and Saviour Jesus Christ." The following excerpts are taken from the fourth lecture.

"Conscious of many shortcomings, a human teacher must at some time relieve his natural sense of honesty, his fundamental instinct of justice, by noting the discrepancy between his weak, imperfect, perhaps miserable self, and his sublime and awful message.... But Jesus Christ makes no approach to such a distinction between Himself and His message. . . . The greatest of the prophets is permitted to see the glory of the Lord, and he forthwith exclaims in agony, 'Woe is me! for I am undone; because I am a man of unclean lips....' Yet Jesus Christ never confesses sin; He never once asks for pardon.... He does not bequeath to His Apostles the task of elaborating a theory respecting the Personal rank of their Master in the scale of being.... He speaks of Himself as the Light of a darkened world, as the

Way by which man may ascend to heaven, as the Truth which can readily satisfy the cravings of the soul, as the Life which must be imparted to all who would live in very deed, to all who would really live forever. . . . He is the Bread of Life. He is the Living Bread that came down from the heaven; believers in Him will feed on Him and have eternal life. . . . All who came before Him He characterizes as having been, by comparison with Himself, the thieves and robbers of mankind. He is Himself the One Good Shepherd of the souls of men. . . . He is the very Door of the sheepfold. . . . He contrasts Himself with a group of His countrymen as follows: 'Ye are from beneath, I am from above; ye are of this world, I am not of this world.'. . . He distinctly places Himself on terms of equality with the Father. . . . Beyond this assertion . . . is our Lord's revelation of His absolute oneness of Essence with the Father." This is only a small portion of Canon Liddon's presentation.

The Testimonies of Believers

Nathanael: Rabbi, thou art the Son of God: thou art the King of Israel (John 1:49).

Simon Peter: Thou art the Christ, the Son of the living God (Matt. 16:16).

Thomas: My Lord and my God (John 20:28).

Paul: Christ, who is over all, God blessed for ever (Rom. 9:5). For in him dwelleth all the fulness of the Godhead bodily (Col. 2:9).

These New Testament expressions could be multiplied many times, but let us hear the testimony of others.

Charles Wesley:

Jesus, my Lord, my God,
The God supreme Thou art;
The Lord of hosts, Whose precious blood
Is sprinkled on my heart.

Justin: But if you knew, Trypho, who He is that is called at one time the Angel of great counsel, and a Man by Ezekiel, and like the Son of man by Daniel, and a Child by Isaiah, and Christ and God to be worshipped by David, . . . you would not have blasphemed Him who has now come, and been born, and suffered, and ascended to heaven; who shall also come again, and then your twelve tribes shall mourn (*Dialogue with Trypho,* cxxvi).

Epiphanius: We believe . . . in one Lord Jesus Christ, the Son of God, . . . God of God, Light of Light, very God of very God, begotten, not made, being of one substance with the Father (*Creed of Epiphanius,* Second Formula).

Augustine: For the Son of God He was—ever the son of God—Creator even of themselves who spoke to Him . . . He is David's Lord then as being God. David's Lord, as being Lord of all (Sermon I on "New Testament Lessons").

Chrysostom on "In the beginning was the Word": Seest thou true philosophy and divine doctrines? Not like those of the Greeks, who assign times, and say that some indeed of the gods are younger, some elder. There is nothing of this with us. For if God Is, as certainly He Is, then nothing was before Him. If He is Creator of all things, He must be first; if Master and Lord of all, then all, both creatures and ages, are after Him (*Homilies on St. John*).

Isaac Watts:

1. Dearest of all the names above,
   My Jesus and my God!
   Who can resist thy heav'nly love,
   Or trifle with thy blood?
2. 'Tis by the merits of thy death
   The Father smiles again;
   'Tis by thine interceding breath
   The Spirit dwells with men.
3. Till God in human flesh I see,
   My thoughts no comfort find;
   The holy, just and sacred Three,
   Are terrors to my mind.
4. But if Immanuel's face appear,
   My hope, my joy begins;
   His name forbids my slavish fear,
   His grace removes my sins.
5. While Jews on their own law rely,
   And Greeks of wisdom boast,
   I love th' incarnate mystery,
   And there I fix my trust.

Impartial Testimonies

Pilate: I find in him no fault at all (John 18:38). I am innocent of the blood of this just person (Matt. 27:24).

The Centurion: Truly this was the Son of God

(Matt. 27:54). Certainly this was a righteous man (Luke 23:47).

Napoleon (to General Bertrand, an avowed unbeliever): I know men; and I tell you that Jesus Christ is not a man. Superficial minds see a resemblance between Christ and the founders of empires, and the gods of other religions. That resemblance does not exist.... We can say to the authors of every other religion, "You are neither gods, nor the agents of the Deity."... What do these gods, so boastful, know more than other mortals... these priests of India or of Memphis; this Confucius; this Mohammed?—absolutely nothing. They have made a perfect chaos of mortals. . . . It is not so with Christ.... He is truly a being by Himself.... In every other existence but that of Christ, how many imperfections!... If you do not perceive that Jesus Christ is God, very well: then I did wrong to make you a general (from John S. C. Abbott's *Life of Napoleon*).

Goethe: I consider the Gospels to be thoroughly genuine, for in them there is the effective reflection of a sublimity which emanated from the Person of Christ; and this is as *Divine* as ever Divine appeared on earth (*Gesprache mit Eckermann*).

John Stuart Mill: And whatever may be taken away from us by rational criticism, Christ is still left; a unique figure, not more unlike his precursors than all his followers, even those who had the direct benefit of his personal teaching. It is of no use to say that Christ as exhibited in the Gospels is not historical.... Who among his disciples or among their proselytes was capable of inventing the sayings ascribed to Jesus, or imagining the life and character revealed in the Gospels?... But about the life and sayings of Jesus there is a stamp of personal originality combined with profundity of insight, which, if we abandon the idle expectation of finding scientific precision where something very different was aimed at, must place the Prophet of Nazareth, even in the estimation of those who have no belief in his inspiration, in the very first rank of the men of sublime genius of whom our species can boast (Essay on "Theism," completed shortly before his death).

The Karaite *Afendopolo* (Caleb b. Elijah b. Judah, died around 1499 A.D.): He was, according to the opinion of the lovers of truth, a wise man, pious, righteous, God-fearing, and shunning evil. Neither did he ever teach any law of practice contrary to the written law.

Samuel Krauss, Ph.D.: However, a great historic movement of the character and importance of Christianity can not have arisen without a great personality to call it into existence and to give it shape and direction. Jesus of Nazareth had a mission from God (see Maimonides, "Yad," Melakim, xi. 4, and other passages quoted in the *Jewish Encyclopedia*, iv. 56 *et seq., s.v.* "Christianity"); and he must have had the spiritual power and fitness to be chosen for it. The very legends surrounding his life and his death furnish proofs of the greatness of his character, and of the depth of the impression which he left upon the people among whom he moved (*The Jewish En-*

cyclopedia, article on "Jesus of Nazareth").

Rabbi Max Merritt of Portland, Oregon (in a published sermon entitled "What Do Jews Think of Jesus?"): Reform rabbis everywhere yield him his due as a spiritual genius, as a man the beauty of whose character can not help making an irresistible appeal. Liberal Jews accord him a deserved place among the noblest teachers and heroes of the faith that Israel produced. We have nothing but pride in this man of our blood and race who enriched the literature of the world with such a gem as the Sermon on the Mount. We too admire this gentle teacher of purity and nobility, this friend of the poor and outcast, the comforter of the fallen and forsaken. We recognize him not only as one of our flesh and blood, but also of the spirit of the prophets—this man who sought to raise men to a higher plane of truth and right.

Back again to *Pilate*: What shall I do with Jesus which is called Christ?

THE DISTINCTIVE BOOK OF CHRISTIANITY

Not any of the sacred literature of the world's religions has been subject to the scrutiny and the criticism as well as the praise that has been accorded the Bible. Those who have condemned it have come and gone, but the Word continues forever settled in heaven (Ps. 119:89).

Let us take Thomas Paine as an example. He completed his *Age of Reason* in 1795. The objections he raised to the Scriptures were those of the English and French deists, but he was out of his realm and lacked the knowledge needed for critical inquiry. In the *New York Tribune* the following statement appeared on March 25, 1876: "His best arguments, if they may be so called, would not, if first published today, attract the slightest attention, nor would anybody think them worthy of serious refutation.... He was an infidel without science, erudition or philosophy. He was simply a sharp debater, a caviller, and a technical disputant...." It was, in fact, this very book of Thomas Paine that started the infidel David Nelson to review his own objections to the Christian religion. He wrote in his book *The Cause of Infidelity* that "the writings of Paine drove me further from his belief than I had ever been.... I read it and could not say that I had found in it either suavity or philanthropy, dignity or sublimity, honesty or truth, but the opposite of them all—the opposite, although the writer was a man of talents..." (pages 292–293). Paine's work has been refuted time and again by men like Bishop Watson in his work *An Apology*, by Thomas Scott in his response to Paine, and by J. Auchinclose, Elias Boudinot, John Disney, Samuel Drew, J. P. Estlin, David Levi, W. McNeill, Thomas Meek, William Patten, David Simpson and John Tytler, to mention only a few.

The reason the Bible has withstood the assaults of its critics is because it is in truth what it claims to be, the Word of God, and men down through the centuries have found it to be so. To the Thessalonians Paul wrote, "For this cause also thank we God without ceasing because, when ye received the word of

God which ye heard from us, ye received it not as the word of men, but, as it is in truth, the word of God. . ." (I Thess. 2: 13). Time and again Paul gave the source of his teaching: "For this we say unto you by the word of the Lord. . ." (I Thess. 4: 15), "For I have received of the Lord that which also I delivered unto you. . ." (I Cor. 11: 23), "For I delivered unto you first of all that which I also received. . ." (I Cor. 15: 3), "For I neither received it of man, neither was I taught it, but by the revelation of Jesus Christ" (Gal. 1: 12). Paul had a reason for being so specific. He explains this in I Corinthians 2 when he states, "That your faith should not stand in the wisdom of men, but in the power of God" (vs. 5). He disclaimed the use of man's wisdom (vs. 4). He knew Hellenism and contrasted his own teaching with it (I Cor. 1: 22, 23).

What background there was to his teaching is not to be found in the various religions of the world but in the sacred Scriptures of Israel themselves. For further study along this line see *Christian Origins and Judaism* by W. D. Davies (Westminster Press), especially chapter VII, "Paul and the Dead Sea Scrolls," and chapter VIII, "A New View of Paul" (based on Professor Munck's *Paulus und die Heilgeschichte*); *Paul, a Study in Social and Religious History* by Adolf Deissmann (Hodder and Stoughton); *The Origin of Paul's Religion* by J. Gresham Machen (Eerdmans); and particularly *Paul and Jesus* by H. N. Ridderbos (Baker Book House).

Dr. Herman Ridderbos became professor of New Testament Studies in the Theological Seminary at

Kampen, the Netherlands, in 1943. In this book he says, "The affirmation of Bultmann, and others, that the synoptic description of Jesus as the Son of God followed the pattern of the god-men . . . known to Hellenism, not only touches the very heart of the historical trustworthiness of the synoptic gospels, but, as has been demonstrated extensively by J. Bieneck, is entirely in conflict with the character of the divine sonship ascribed to Jesus in the synoptic gospels."

For further evidence of the distinctive claim of the Bible to divine inspiration the student should study the following Scriptures:

1. Expressions such as "the Lord said," "the Lord spake," "the word of the Lord came," occur between two and three thousand times. One estimate is 2,601 times: 680 in the books of Moses, 196 in the Poetical books, 418 in the Historical books, 1,307 in the Prophetical books. Another estimate gives a total of 3,808.

2. The writers were conscious that what they were speaking and writing was commanded by God: Exodus 24:4; II Samuel 23:2 (note the exactness of this claim—"The Spirit of the Lord spake by me, and his word was in my tongue"); Jeremiah 1:7, 9; 30:1; Habakkuk 2:2; I Corinthians 2:13; 14:37; I Thessalonians 2:13; I Timothy 4:1; I Peter 1:11, 12.

3. The writers were conscious that what the others had written was commanded by God: Joshua 8:31; Nehemiah 8:1; Daniel 9:2; Zechariah 7:12 (note especially the force of this: ". . . the words which the Lord of hosts hath sent by his Spirit by the

former prophets"); Malachi 4:4; Luke 1:70; Acts 1:16; II Peter 1:21; 3:15, 16.

4. It is specifically stated that the writers were given the very words: Zechariah 7:12; I Corinthians 2:13; I Thessalonians 2:13.

5. The Holy Spirit is expressly said to have spoken the words that were written: Mark 12:36; Acts 1:16; 4:25, American Standard Version; Acts 28:25; Hebrews 3:7; 9:8; 10:15.

6. The Lord Jesus Christ placed the stamp of eternity upon His own words: Matthew 24:35; Mark 13:31; Luke 21:33.

7. The Lord Jesus Christ verified the claim of the Pentateuch to be the very word that came from the mouth of God: Deuteronomy 8:3; Matthew 4:4.

8. The Lord Jesus Christ guaranteed to His disciples the Holy Spirit's assistance in recalling the very words He spoke: John 14:26.

9. The Apostle Peter set forth the full inspiration of Scripture and definitely asserted that it did not come by human will but was the direct work of the Holy Spirit: II Peter 1:20, 21. The word "moved" means far more than the giving of an impulse. The Greek word is *phero,* to bear or carry. This is more than guiding, controlling, or even directing. Warfield, in the *International Standard Bible Encyclopedia,* has the following pointed comment: "What is 'borne' is taken up by the 'bearer,' and conveyed by the 'bearer's' power, not its own, to the 'bearer's' goal, not its own. The men who spoke from God are here declared, therefore, to have been taken up by the Holy Spirit and brought by His power to the goal

of His choosing. The things which they spoke under this operation of the Spirit were therefore His things, not theirs."

10. The Apostle Peter claimed that the very word which the apostles were preaching was the eternal word of the Lord: I Peter 1:25. This was even then being put into writing.

11. The necessary fulfillment of every detail of Scripture manifests its total Divine origin: Matthew 1:22; 2:15; 26:54; Mark 9:12, 13; 14:49; Luke 24:25, 44; John 13:18.

12. The expression "it is written" introduces between eighty and ninety Old Testament quotations in the New Testament. What is written becomes the test of action, the foundation of doctrine, the extent of revealed truth: Matthew 2:5; Mark 14:21; Luke 19:46; John 6:45; Acts 23:5; Romans 1:17; I Corinthians 9:9; II Corinthians 8:15; Galatians 3:10; Hebrews 10:7; I Peter 1:16.

13. There is an evident claim to verbal communication in the way many quotations from the Old Testament are introduced as having been spoken *through* the prophets: Matthew 2:5, 15, 17; 3:3; 4:14; 12:17; 13:35; 21:4; Acts 2:16; 28:25.

14. The Holy Spirit is clearly set forth as the teacher of the very words that should be spoken: Matthew 10:20; Luke 12:11, 12.

15. The words of Scripture are used with exact precision and discrimination. The argument of Galatians 3:16 turns upon the use of the singular instead of the plural number; Galatians 4:9 upon the passive rather than the active voice; John 10:34–36 upon

the inviolability of a single word; Hebrews 12:27 upon the phrase "yet once more." (This line of evidence we found suggested by Dr. A. T. Pierson in *Knowing the Scriptures.*)

16. So sacred does God hold His word that man was forbidden to add to it or alter it: Deuteronomy 4:2; 12:32; Proverbs 30:6; Jeremiah 26:2; I Corinthians 4:6; Revelation 22:18, 19.

17. Finally, let it be remembered that there is a terrible curse upon all who refuse to recognize and obey the word of God: Isaiah 5:24; 30:12, 13.

The matter indicated under point 11 is one of the most important distinctive features of the Old and New Testaments—one which is not to be found in the writings of any other of the world's religions. It has been estimated that the prophetic element constitutes thirty-four percent of the entire contents of Scripture. But it is not the fact of prophecy only which is unique. *It is the fact that the Bible itself makes the fulfillment of prophecy the test and proof of its own validity* (Deut. 18:20–22). No other work to which the ascription of "sacred literature" is given makes, or could make, this claim. To this might be added the miraculous feature of the *unity* of the Word, which applies not only to its history and doctrine but to prophecy as well. What gives such strong evidential force to this matter of unity is the fact that the sixty-six books were written over a period of almost two thousand years by men of different backgrounds, abilities, and from a variety of geographical locations.

THE DISTINCTIVE DOCTRINE OF CHRISTIANITY

The basic doctrine of the Christian faith upon which all the others rest is that of the tri-unity of God. The theological expression for this is "trinity," from the Latin *trini,* three each or threefold. The doctrine is sometimes assailed on the ground that the word "trinity" does not occur in the Bible, but the argument is superficial. Words such as omnipresent, omnipotent, and omniscient are also not in the Bible—but the truth they signify is taught there. So it is with the concept of the Trinity.

This doctrine, like certain others such as sacrifice and the virgin birth, may be traced in some of the ancient religions in one form or another but never in its distinctive Biblical presentation. However, this is to be expected on the basis of Paul's statement in Romans 1:21–28 that men at one time knew God but glorified Him not as God and changed the truth of God into a lie. Polytheism, instead of being a step in the evolutionary ascent of man, is set forth here as exactly the reverse. Man degraded into it. If one were not to find remnants of early Scripture teaching in the non-Biblical religions, the critics would have been the first to assail the Word on this ground as demonstrating that it had no antiquity. Now, their only recourse is to say that it borrowed from them.

Adam Clarke concludes his comments on the first chapter of John's Gospel with a series of testimonies from the Chaldee Targums, the Zend Avesta,

Philo, etc., concerning the Logos. He then states: "It is remarkable that *Moses* and the *prophets*, the ancient *Chaldee Targumists*, the author or authors of the *Zend Avesta, Plato* and the first philosophers of Greece, *Philo* the Jew, *John* and the *apostles*, and perhaps even *Mohammed* himself, should all so perfectly coincide in their ideas concerning a glorious person in the Godhead!"

In giving his testimonies concerning the Trinity he has some extracts from *Lettre sur les Characteres Chinois*, 4to. Bruxelles, 1773, of which the following is significant to students of Comparative Religion. "Among the *ancient* Chinese characters which have been preserved, we find the following △ like the Greek *delta*. . . . According to the Chinese dictionary *Kang-hi*, this character signifies *union*. According to *Choueouen*, a celebrated work, △ is *three united in one*. The *Lieou chou tsing hoen*, which is a rational and learned explanation of ancient characters, says: '△ signifies intimate union, harmony, the chief good of man, of the heaven, and of earth; it is the *union of three*.' The book *Se-ki* says, 'Formerly the emperor made a solemn sacrifice every three years to the Spirit Trinity in Unity.'. . ."

We saw under Taoism that although *Tao* originally meant "way" it came to signify *impersonal divinity*. Adam Clarke gives the following quotation from the text of Lao-Tze, where some influence of the doctrine of the trinity might be traced. "He who is as visible, and yet cannot be seen, is denominated *lieou;* he who can be heard, and yet speaks not to the ears, *hi;* he who is as tangible, and yet cannot be felt, is named *ouci*: in vain do you consult your *senses* concerning these *three;* your *reason* alone can discover them, and it will tell you that they are *one*: above, there is no light; below, no darkness. He is eternal. There is no name which can designate him. He bears no similitude to any created thing. He is an *image* without *form;* and a *form* without *matter*. His light is encompassed in darkness.... What *Tao* has always been, such he continues to be: for he is eternal, and the commencement of wisdom."

Although the eternity and wisdom of God are here set forth, the Scriptures tell us further that God is light, and in Him is no darkness at all (I John 1:5). They present a God who has manifested himself to His creatures both in nature (Rom. 1:20) and in man (Gen. 1:26) and by very incarnation in the Lord Jesus Christ himself (I Tim. 3:16). The tri-unity of the Godhead is revealed not as merely a threefold manifestation but as three distinct persons who are, nevertheless, one in essence, each possessing all the divine attributes. This unity is so complete as to be an absolute monotheism and yet so constituted that God the Father could send God the Son to die for the sin of the world. So marvelous is this unity that, instead of the incarnation violating it, we are told that "in him dwelleth all the fulness of the Godhead bodily" (Col. 2:9).

Our term "tri-unity" is based, first of all, upon the use of *'echad* in Deuteronomy 6:4—which means a compound unity of two or more—and then upon the fact that this unity is shown to consist of three persons (as in Isaiah 48:12–16). In Romans 1:20

Paul uses the creation of the *kosmos* as demonstrating this Godhead (*theiotes*). The universe (*unus*, one, plus *vertere*, turn; turned into one, combined in one whole) is an absolute tri-unity of space, time, and matter. Each of these in turn is an absolute tri-unity. Space consists of length, breadth, and depth or height; time is future, present, past; matter is energy, motion, and phenomena. Here we have not merely an illustration of three in one—as in the case of the light, heat, and ultra-violet rays of the sunbeam or the manifestation of H_2O as liquid, ice, and steam—but an absolute tri-unity composed of three absolute tri-unities. In the light of this Paul rightly concludes that man is without excuse. Surely, God was in Christ reconciling the world unto Himself, and He who knew no sin was made to be sin for us that we might be made the righteousness of God in Him (II Cor. 5:21).

Bibliography

Chapter One

Cyclopaedia of Biblical, Theological and Ecclesiastical Literature, M'Clintock and Strong, 12 volumes, 1895, Harper and Brothers, New York

History of Religion, Allan Menzies, 4th edition, revised 1927, Charles Scribner's Sons, New York

Schaff-Herzog Encyclopedia of Religious Knowledge, 3rd edition, revised 1891, Funk and Wagnalls Company, New York

The World's Living Religions, Robert E. Hume, 1924, revised 1947, Charles Scribner's Sons, New York

The World's Religions, Edited by J. N. D. Anderson, 3rd edition, 1955, Wm. B. Eerdmans Publishing Company, Grand Rapids, Michigan

Chapters Two and Three

The Babylonian Talmud, translated into English with notes under the editorship of Rabbi Dr. I. Epstein,

1948, The Soncino Press Limited, London

Everyman's Talmud, A. Cohen, 1949, E. P. Dutton and Company, Inc., New York

The English Hexapla, Samuel Bagster and Sons, London

The Hymns of the Rigveda, Translated by Ralph T. H. Griffith, 4 volumes, 1899, E. J. Lazarus Company, Benares

The Jewish Encyclopedia, 1906, Funk and Wagnalls, New York and London

The Koran, Translated by George Sale, 1880, American Book Exchange, New York

Sacred Books of the East, 49 volumes, 1879–1894, Index Volume 50, 1910, The Claredon Press, Oxford

The Sacred Writings of the World's Great Religions, Selected and Edited by S. E. Frost, Jr., 1948, The New Home Library Series, The Blakiston Company, Philadelphia, Pennsylvania

Chapter Four

The Ante-Nicene Fathers, 9 volumes, 1885, American Reprint of the Edinburgh Edition, The Christian Literature Publishing Company, Buffalo, New York

The Nicene and Post-Nicene Fathers, 11 volumes, 1887, Edited by Philip Schaff, The Christian Literature Publishing Company, Buffalo, New York

The Creeds of Christendom, 3 volumes, 6th edition, 1931, by Philip Schaff, Harper and Brothers, New York

The Divinity of Our Lord and Saviour Jesus Christ, H. P. Liddon, 1882, Rivingtons, London